ALL THE SCULPTURE OF
**DONATELLO**
Part 2
*VOLUME TWENTY-FOUR*
*in the*
*Complete Library of World Art*

The Complete Library of World A

# ALL THE SCULPTURE

# OF DONATELLO

## Part 2

*By* LUIGI GRASSI

*Translated by* PAUL COLACICCHI

HAWTHORN BOOKS, INC.

*Publishers · New York*

*Printed and bound in Great Britain by Jarrold & Sons Ltd, Norwich*

# CONTENTS

# DONATELLO'S SCULPTURE

## THE DECORATIONS IN THE OLD SACRISTY OF SAN LORENZO

The decoration of the Old Sacristy, built by Brunelleschi, consists of eight bas-reliefs in painted plaster (mostly dark red or white against a blue ground): there are in fact eight *tondi*, with a diameter of 215\*, representing the Four Evangelists, *Matthew*, *John*, *Luke* and *Mark* and four episodes from the legend of St John: *St John on Patmos*; *The Raising of Drusiana*; *The Martyrdom of St John* and *The Ascension of St John*. The eight bas-reliefs were executed for the base of the vault. Two other half-reliefs were set above the doors, within two arched frames (*215 × 180*); they represent two pairs of saints: *Lawrence and Stephen* and *Cosmas and Damian*. By far the most ambitious scheme was, however, the pair of bronze doors (*235 × 109*), each decorated with ten panels, each approximately 1 foot square: the *Door of the Apostles* and the *Door of the Martyrs*. It is almost certain that this work was carried out at the express wish of Cosimo de' Medici between 1435 and 1443. However, the chronological and other problems concerning these decorations are many and extremely complex ones; a complete discussion of the differing opinions may be found in Janson's catalogue. Recently (1958), M. Lisner gave fresh consideration to the matter and particularly to the question of discriminating as accurately as possible between Brunelleschi's original project and Donatello's subsequent intervention, but without coming to any definite conclusion. Lisner attributes to Donatello the *Sepulcher of Giovanni d'Averardo dei Medici and his Wife Piccarda* in the center of the Sacristy, executed by Buggiano between 1429 and 1433. It is reasonable, however, to assume that the eight *tondi* and the two half-reliefs above the bronze doors were finished some time before the doors themselves. There are no direct documents concerning this work, but Donatello's contribution was mentioned by Filarete (around 1464), Antonio Manetti (around 1475), Vespasiano da Bisticci (around 1485), Albertini (1510), Vasari (1550 and 1568) and others.

### Plate 98a

ST MATTHEW. *Tondo.* The ornamented throne on which the saint is seated and the desk in perspective recall the stucco decorations of the Roman interiors in the days of Augustus. Kauffmann has noticed other iconographic analogies with Byzantine miniatures depicting the apostles. A study of the linear and perspective convergences, the vitality, the spiritual and physical energy, the pictorial realization and the dense plastic modeling, are all characteristic of Donatello's innovating and

\* All dimensions are given in centimeters.

### Plate 98b

ST JOHN. *Tondo*. The Evangelist in this relief is calm and meditative, but his drapery has a restless and dynamic pictorial quality strongly contrasting with the composition of his throne and desk.

### Plate 99a

ST LUKE. *Tondo*. This, of the four Evangelist reliefs, is perhaps the most inspired and successful.

### Plate 99b

ST MARK. *Tondo*.

### Plate 100a

ST JOHN ON PATMOS. *Tondo*. A beautifully imagined, fantastic bas-relief—tinted in white and dark red against a blue ground—from the story of John the Evangelist.

### Plate 100b

THE RAISING OF DRUSIANA. *Tondo*. This illustration from the same cycle is clearly dominated by the architectural perspective.

### Plate 101a

THE MARTYRDOM OF ST JOHN. *Tondo*. The third episode from the cycle of John the Evangelist, is probably the most illustrative of the eight reliefs, and by far the least convincing of the whole sequence. The saint is praying as he stands half-immersed in a cauldron of boiling oil, inside a castle, against a background of towers and battlements. It is interesting to observe that a *tondo*, for Donatello, does not necessarily mean a round composition. It can be any image geometrically inscribed within the base

of the visual pyramid, so that the circle's curve cuts across figures and objects.

### Plate 101b

THE ASCENSION OF ST JOHN. *Tondo*. The architectural structures rising in perspective cubes represent the final episode of the *St John* cycle. Parronchi (1959) commented on this *tondo* in the course of studying Brunelleschi's famous perspective tables. Parronchi holds that Donatello applied to the *tondo* of the *Ascension* the principle of "perspective construction as developed upon points of distance." This principle has been previously used by Brunelleschi in his conception of the Piazza della Signoria in Florence, but here Donatello places his imaginary skyline much below the *tondo*'s lower limit. In the other three *tondi* it more or less coincides with the picture's horizontal diameter. For Parronchi, as for Sampaolesi (1950), these *Legends of St John* are probably the first reliefs executed by Donatello in the Sacristy, before, that is, the journey to Rome. For this reason they are still strictly consistent with Brunelleschi's perspective principles and with the general architecture of the Sacristy. The disagreement with Brunelleschi, therefore, must have taken place because of Donatello's Bronze Doors.

### Plate 102a

SS COSMAS AND DAMIAN. Stucco relief above the pediment of the *Door of the Apostles*. Believed by Janson to be the earliest decorative element contributed by Donatello to the Brunelleschi Sacristy, and to have been executed in 1434–35. We refer nonetheless, to the estimated date of the stucco decorations as a whole, that is, between 1435 and 1443.

94

## Plate 102b

SS STEPHEN AND LAWRENCE. Stucco relief above the pediment of the *Door of the Martyrs*. Also datable between 1435 and 1443.

## Plate 103a

DOOR OF THE APOSTLES. *Bas-reliefs, bronze, in 10 squares, 31 × 30 each.* They are divided by frames and represent paired Apostles against a flat background. The measurement of the whole door is 235 × 109. Both doors were executed by Donatello probably between 1440 and 1443, a considerable time after the stucco decorations. They were restored in 1946–47 by Bruno Bearzi, who eliminated from the bronze surfaces the incrustation which gave an impression of slovenly or inexperienced casting and chasing. Donatello's *Apostles* were a departure from Alberti's classical decor, and described as "fencers" by Filarete. The plate shows a general view of this door. See details of the 10 squares in plates 104a–108b.

## Plate 103b

DOOR OF THE MARTYRS. Bas-reliefs, bronze, in 10 squares, 31 × 39 each, divided by frames and representing paired Martyrs against a flat background. The measurement of the whole door is also 235 × 109. Probably executed between 1440 and 1443. Kauffmann (1935) observed that the frames in this door are noticeably wider than those in the *Door of the Apostles*. As a result the squares are smaller and for this reason the paired *Martyrs* seem to take up more room. The plate shows a general view. See details of the 10 squares in plates 109a–113b.

## Plate 104a

DOOR OF THE APOSTLES. Detail: the first square on the left, with St John the Baptist with an Evangelist.

## Plate 104b

DOOR OF THE APOSTLES. Detail: the first square on the right, with St Peter (at the left, with a key) and St Paul (at the right, with a sword).

## Plate 105a

DOOR OF THE APOSTLES. Detail: the second square on the left, with two Apostles. The Apostle on the left, carrying a cross, is presumably St Andrew.

## Plate 105b

DOOR OF THE APOSTLES. Detail: the second square on the right, with the Doctors of the Church discussing a sacred text.

## Plate 106a

DOOR OF THE APOSTLES. Detail: the third square on the left. Two Evangelists, or Doctors of the Church, are seen discussing the Holy Scriptures.

## Plate 106b

DOOR OF THE APOSTLES. Detail: the third square on the right. Two saints are engaged in a heated discussion about the interpretation of the Holy Scriptures. This relief by Donatello was copied by Antonio da Sangallo in one of his drawings.

## Plate 107a

DOOR OF THE APOSTLES. Detail: the fourth square on the left.

## Plate 107b

DOOR OF THE APOSTLES. Detail: the fourth square on the right. An almost heraldic representation of two Apostles writing at a desk.

### Plate 108a

DOOR OF THE APOSTLES. Detail: the fifth square on the left. Two Doctors of the Church. The Apostle at the left, with a bishop's crook and miter, could be St Augustine.

### Plate 108b

DOOR OF THE APOSTLES. Detail: the fifth square on the right. Two saints, a pope and a bishop are represented.

### Plate 109a

DOOR OF THE MARTYRS. Detail: the first square on the left. The two martyrs here are clearly identifiable as St Stephen and St Lawrence.

### Plate 109b

DOOR OF THE MARTYRS. Detail: the first square on the right. Two martyrs.

### Plate 110a

DOOR OF THE MARTYRS. Detail: the second square on the left. Two saints move towards each other. The palms of their martyrdom are crossed like two swords.

### Plate 110b

DOOR OF THE MARTYRS. Detail: the second square on the right. Once again, though in a quieter debate, the palms of martyrdom are almost crossed, thus justifying Filarete's description of "fencers."

### Plate 111a

DOOR OF THE MARTYRS. Detail: the third square on the left. We see here Donatello's feeling for pictorial movement.

### Plate 111b

DOOR OF THE MARTYRS. Detail: the third square on the right. The two figures are in unusual poses, though they become united at the center, where their books come together creating a kind of geometrical pattern. The two palms are held in such a way as to create the impression of an open fan.

### Plate 112a

DOOR OF THE MARTYRS. Detail: the fourth square on the left. The martyr at the left gestures towards the other, who is leaning against the frame, perhaps to concentrate before he begins to write.

### Plate 112b

DOOR OF THE MARTYRS. Detail: the fourth square on the right. The two martyrs, one of whom is leaning against the frame, appear to have interrupted briefly—rather than concluded—their theological argument.

### Plate 113a

DOOR OF THE MARTYRS. Detail: the fifth square on the left. These two saints appear to be dancing, if not sparring, in the course of their debate.

### Plate 113b

DOOR OF THE MARTYRS. Detail: the fifth square on the right. The two martyrs turn away from each other, possibly to indicate that their dialogue, as well as the sequence, is now concluded.

## Plate 114

ST LEONARD. *Terracotta bust, 50 × 52. Florence, Old Sacristy of San Lorenzo.* No trace of polychromy. No documented history. This work was once more commonly known as a *Bust of St Lawrence.* Domenico Moreni (1813) was the first to describe it as *St Leonard,* and it was located originally in the Neroni Chapel in San Lorenzo, where it was used as a reliquary. In his essay on the chapel's architecture, W. Paatz (1933) confirmed Moreni's identification and dated the bust (generally thought to have been finished by Donatello in or about 1440) "after 1457," that is, after the sculptor's stay in Padua. This theory was accepted by Kauffmann (1935). Later, however, the *St Leonard* was excluded altogether from the body of Donatello's autograph works by Lányi and Planiscig. More recently Janson (1957), though he could not accept the attribution to Donatello, acknowledged the very high quality of the bust and suggested it be ascribed to Desiderio. We do not think that its original location in the Beroni Chapel should affect the question of dating it. The *St Leonard* bust is a lyrically characterized portrait of a youth, and its sculptural style is consistent with the decorations in the Old Sacristy, particularly the relief of *SS Stephen and Lawrence* above the Door of the Martyrs (plate 102b). Nor do we believe that the master's stay in Padua preceded this work; it certainly does not seem to have affected it. In fact the bust has an ascetic "content" which does not fit with Donatello's late period. There seems to be no valid reason why it should not be unreservedly claimed for Donatello. The plate shows the right profile of the whole bust. See also plate 115.

## Plate 115

ST LEONARD. Front view.

## Plate 116

DAVID. *Bronze statuette, height 37. Berlin, Staatliches Museen.* This statuette was long thought to be a preparatory work for the Martelli *David* (plates 64–67), from a previous model in wax. If this were so, the work would have been done about 1430. The style and pose of this figure admittedly recall the Martelli *David,* but its representational manner and modeling are extremely different from the larger masterpiece. We should not be misled by the apparently sketchy aspect of this little bronze, which, far from being a model for the Martelli statue, is a fresh and later interpretation of it, executed by Donatello himself.

We find here the same pictorial boldness that we saw in the bronze doors of the San Lorenzo Sacristy. Kauffmann (1935) was quick to notice the relationship between the Berlin *David* and the San Lorenzo doors ("*schon in die Nähe der Bronzetüren in der Alten Sakristei von San Lorenzo führt*"). He did not, however, draw any logical conclusion from his discovery, and continued to consider the bronze statuette as a model for the Martelli *David.* Planiscig (1947) removed the Berlin figure from his catalogue of Donatello's works. Here Planiscig obviously had changed his mind, for in a previous essay, which he wrote in 1930, he described the statuette as a "small wax model for the Martelli *David.*" Janson (1957) has twice rejected the attribution to Donatello of this work which he ascribes to a minor artist. We disagree.

## Plate 117

BUST OF YOUTH (called SON OF GATTAMELATA). *Bronze bust, 42×42. Florence, Bargello.* Surely this was the portrait of a Florentine contemporary, possibly a member of the Medici court, finished by Donatello (in our view) shortly before he went to Padua, perhaps in 1443. The oval cameo medallion on the young man's chest shows the chariot of Platonic love, a fact which would seem to confirm the bust's aulic, humanistic and Neo-Platonic origins, as correctly indicated by Wittkower (1937–38). Donatello was quite capable of expressing, especially in portrait-sculpture, the ideals of the academic and Neo-Platonic *milieu* of the Medici court. On the other hand the quality of this bust is so high, the face so noble and thoughtful, the lineaments so consonant with Donatello's manner that we claim it unreservedly for the master.

The attribution was rejected by Schmarsow (1889) and Semrau (1891). More recently Lányi (1939) and André Chastel (1950) analyzed it more closely. Chastel observes that the bust's style, markedly archaizing, and the proclaimed Neo-Platonic associations of the sitter are incompatible with Donatello and reflect Ficino's clear influence on the anonymous sculptor. In other words the bust, in Chastel's views, could be a late Desiderio or a Mino da Fiesole, and could not possibly have been executed before 1475. H. W. Janson again, on the strength of new arguments, assigned the bust to Donatello. The execution, in Janson's view, took place in or about 1440.

## Plate 118

CRUCIFIX. *Bronze statue, 176×170. Padua, Basilica of St Anthony, Altar of the Saint.* This figure was executed for a cross formerly placed in the middle of the church, perhaps between the columns holding the pulpit and the one opposite. There it remained until December 1486, when, for reasons of space, it was removed to the center of the entrance to the choir and stood upon a marble pedestal. Later (1651–52), the choir screen was demolished and the *Crucifix* became part of a great baroque altar. In 1895, Boito arbitrarily reconstructed Donatello's *Altar of the Saint*, and placed the *Crucifix* among the statues which adorned it.

We know that on January 24, 1444, Donatello had received the metal for casting it. The few and meager documents available do not allow us to trace in detail the development of this work and the chronology of the various operations of modeling, casting and cleaning. It appears, however, that in July, 1445, Donatello had still not delivered the *Crucifix*, the balance for which was not paid until June 23, 1449. Meanwhile, in January 1449, Nicolò Pizzolo had been paid for having painted and gilded the wood cross for Donatello's *Crucifix*, and Andrea dalle Caldiere had been remunerated for a copper diadem he executed, also for the *Crucifix*. (This diadem was immediately gilded by Bartolomeo de Castagnaro.) The loincloth worn by Christ is a baroque addition. The documents relating to this work and to the *Altar of the Saint* in Padua were published by A. Gloria (*Donatello Fiorentino e le sue opere mirabili nel tempio di Sant'Antonio di Padova*, Padua, 1895). More recently P. Antonio Sartori republished the records with comment (*Documenti riguardanti Donatello e il suo altare di*

*Padova*, Padua, 1961). The plate
shows a front view of the whole
*Crucifix*. See also plate 119.

Plate 119
CRUCIFIX. Detail: the bust and
head.

# THE ALTAR OF THE SAINT IN PADUA

The High Altar of St Anthony, in the Basilica of Sant'Antonio in Padua, is made up of twenty-nine sculptures: seven bronze statues (*Enthroned Madonna and Child, St Francis, St Anthony, St Daniel, St Justina, St Louis* and *St Prosdocimus*); four bronze reliefs representing the *Miracles of St Anthony* (*Miracle of the Mule, Miracle of the Speaking Babe, Miracle of the Healing of the Penitent Son, Miracle of the Miser's Heart*); four bronze reliefs representing the *Symbols of the Evangelists* (Matthew, John, Mark and Luke); one bronze relief of a *Pietà*; twelve small

Boito's reconstruction

99

Kauffmann's reconstruction

rectangular bronze reliefs of *Singing and Musician Angels*; a large panel of the *Entombment of Christ* in stone. To these should be added, in the opinion of Fiocco, two stone fragments representing the half-figures of two *Doctors of the Church*. The altar's history, so far as its architecture and original sculptures are concerned, goes back to 1446 (see "Biographical Notes") and up to 1450. June 13, 1448 is an important date, because then the feast of St Anthony is traditionally celebrated, and the bronze reliefs and the statues were temporarily placed around and on a wooden altar standing on eight columns. This first architectural

projection of the *Altar* he later modified to include the *Musician Angels*, the bronze *Pietà*, the panel of the *Entombment*, and also an *Eternal Father* and four marble reliefs. The altar was also decorated in the front and rear. The architectural framework of the structure must have had multi-colored elements, beginning with the different hues of marble, bronze and other decorations. Unfortunately, we do not know its original composition, because the basic structure was demolished (the sculptures have been preserved) between 1579 and 1582 to make room for a new altar built by Gerolamo Campagna and

Cesare Franco. In 1668, the later altar was also radically changed and Donatello's statues were placed around the Basilica. A first reconstruction of the original arrangement, by Boito (1895)—a diagram of which is reproduced on page 99—was both aesthetically and historically wrong. The most interesting modern reconstructions are by Cordenons, Von Hadeln, Fiocco, Kauffmann, Band, Planiscig, Janson and again Fiocco. In fact any such attempt can only be based upon two references: a statement by Marcantonio Michiel, who died in 1552, and Nicolò Pizzolo's eye-witness account. Even though it does not deal with the whole work, the latter is to be considered a fundamental document. He wrote: "In the Church of the Santo, above the main altar, are four rounded figures in bronze around a statue of Our Lady. Below these figures on the retable are four bronze reliefs, two in the front and two in the back, representing 'little stories' and at the sides are four other bronze reliefs depicting the Evangelists. These, however, are only half-figures. Behind the altar, beneath the retable, is the dead Christ with other figures around Him, and two more figures on the right and two on the left; there are marble reliefs by the hand of Donatello." Of course, in this book, we are interested only in Donatello as a sculptor but the *Altar of the Saint* has to be considered as an architectural and plastic work taken as a whole. In his reconstruction, Planiscig (removing the

Janson's reconstruction

Fiocco's reconstruction (front view)

statues of *St Ludovic* and *St Prosdocimus*, and placing them by the corners of the steps), was entirely guided by Michiel, who mentions only four bronze figures standing on a pedestal upon the altar. Kauffmann, however (1935), and Janson (1957), considering Michiel's report to be no more than a fragmentary and none too exact description, believe that all six figures of saints were grouped on either side of the central

Fiocco's reconstruction (back view)

*Madonna and Child* within the general frame of a tabernacle, which thus constituted a coherent altarpiece. But while Kauffmann imagined, and not without reason, that the *Singing and Musician Angels* were arranged vertically along the lateral pilasters, Janson correctly observed that the tabernacle must have been divided into three parts by two pillars, as in the case of Mantegna's *San Zeno Altarpiece* in Verona (generally

Fiocco's reconstruction (side view)

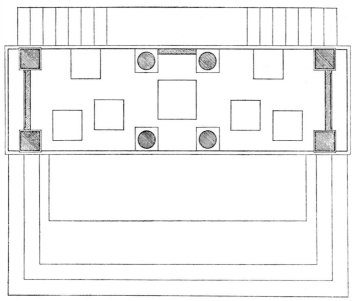

Fiocco's reconstruction (plan)

accepted as an indirect reference for reconstructing Donatello's altar).

A recent and convincing arrangement, however, is suggested by Fiocco (1961) after new and careful thought on the whole problem. Fiocco respected Janson's concept of the altarpiece: four marble pilasters at the corners; four rounded and ribbed pillars of partly gilded marble in the middle; an arched roof with four rounded *orecchioni* at the corners. Two of these latter features were done in stone and decorated with circular patterns of gold and silver. They can now be seen, as Fiocco describes them, above the entrance of the Museo Antoniano in Padua. Fiocco

has also followed Janson's arrangement in placing the *Singing and Musician Angels* on the step just below the statues, but he distributes them differently from the American critic; a group of five angels on each side of the altar and two in front, on each side of the *Pietà*. In Fiocco's version, furthermore, the statues of *St Daniel* and *St Justina* are shown standing at the rear of the altar and gesturing towards the tabernacle behind the *Madonna*; the Virgin is therefore flanked only by the two statues of the *SS Prosdocimus and Louis* at the far ends and by the *SS Francis and Anthony* on each side. These two statues are smaller than those of the bishops, and Fiocco seems to have pushed them back towards the rear of the altar, so that the four figures form in fact a half-circle round the throne. The throne itself rests upon a pedestal; as a result, the seated *Virgin* towers above her attendant *Saints*. The flanks of the altar, in Fiocco's opinion, were enclosed by stone reliefs, representing four half-figures (two on each side) of *Doctors of the Church*, looking out from a kind of parapet: two of these figures, executed by assistants, are recognizable in the two stone fragments in the Museo di Santo Spirito in Florence (see plate 150). Finally the four corner pilasters, on two faces with *schiacciato* reliefs by Nicolò Coccari and his assistants, could be the same as those removed to the Presbytery after the dismemberment of the original altar. Though still there, they had to be almost entirely rebuilt after the fire of 1749. See above, diagrams of the reconstructions by Kauffmann, Janson and Fiocco.

Plate 120

MADONNA AND CHILD. *Bronze statue, height about 160.* It must have been modeled by May, 1448, because although cast but not cleaned, it was placed upon the temporary altar on the following June 13. This purely frontal and hieratic composition is strongly reminiscent of the Byzantine-Romanesque tradition. Its iconographic relationship to an eleventh-century altarpiece in Santa Maria Maggiore in Florence is not unconvincing. The plate shows the front view of the whole statue. See also plates 121–123.

Plate 121

MADONNA AND CHILD. Detail: the Virgin's head.

Plate 122

MADONNA AND CHILD. Detail: the Child.

Plate 123

MADONNA AND CHILD. Detail: Adam and Eve in a relief at the rear of the throne.

Plate 124a

ST FRANCIS. *Bronze statue, height about 150.* Comments concerning this and the other single statues upon Donatello's altar may be found on pages 31–32 of "Life and Work." The plate shows a general view of the whole statue. See also plates 127–128.

Plate 124b

ST ANTHONY. *Bronze statue, approximately 145 in height.* The plate shows a general view of the whole statue. See also plate 129.

Plate 125a

ST DANIEL. *Bronze statue, height about 152.* The plate shows a general view of the statue. See also plate 130.

Plate 125b

ST JUSTINA. *Bronze statue, height about 152.* The plate shows a general view of the statue. See also plate 131.

Plate 126a

ST LOUIS. *Bronze statue, height about 164.* General view.

Plate 126b

ST PROSDOCIMUS. *Bronze statue, approximately 163 in height.* This and the other five figures of saints are included in Michiel's description: ". . . four rounded figures in bronze round a statue of Our Lady. . . ." If his account was accurate, then only two statues on each side flanked the group of the *Madonna and Child*. Such, in fact, is the altar's construction as attempted by Planiscig and—though with a different distribution—by Fiocco. The plate shows a general view of the whole statue. See also plates 132–133.

### Plate 127
ST FRANCIS. Detail: the head.

### Plate 128
ST FRANCIS. Detail: the Crucifix held by the saint.

### Plate 129
ST ANTHONY. Detail: the head.

### Plate 130
ST DANIEL. Detail: the head.

### Plate 131
ST JUSTINA. Detail: the head.

### Plate 132
ST PROSDOCIMUS. Detail: the hands and body.

### Plate 133
ST PROSDOCIMUS. Detail: the head.

### Plate 134
MIRACLE OF THE MULE. *Bronze relief, 57 × 123.* One of the four Miracles sculptured by Donatello for the main altar in Padua, mentioned in records for 1447, May to November. This relief represents the mule refusing food and kneeling in front of the Consecrated Host. Donatello achieves his perspective by establishing a vanishing point well below the heads of the foreground figures and thus increasing the impression of running lines. The three arched vaults may have been inspired by the Basilica of Massentius in Rome and by Alberti's *Sant' Andrea* in Mantua. The plate shows the whole relief. See also plate 138.

### Plate 135
MIRACLE OF THE SPEAKING BABE. *Bronze relief, 57 × 123.* Here the child recognizes his mother. Though the architectural setting is different from that of the previous relief, the vanishing point chosen by Donatello is the same, and the resulting impression of depth remains unchanged. The plate shows the whole relief. See also plate 139.

### Plate 136
MIRACLE OF THE PENITENT SON. *Bronze relief, 57 × 123.* St Anthony heals the leg of the repentant son, who had kicked his mother. Again, the setting is new. We are now confronted with an impressive public stadium. Donatello's inventiveness is inexhaustible. The plate shows the whole relief. See also plates 140–141.

### Plate 137
MIRACLE OF THE MISER'S HEART. *Bronze relief, 57 × 123.* This is known to be the fourth episode cast in bronze on November 15, 1447. St Anthony indicates the body of a miser who has no heart. The heart is found in a coffer containing his treasures. In this case, Donatello was interested in creating a vibrant movement. The plate shows the whole relief. See also plate 142.

### Plate 138
MIRACLE OF THE MULE. Detail: the center.

### Plate 139
MIRACLE OF THE SPEAKING BABE. Detail: figures at the right.

### Plate 140
MIRACLE OF THE PENITENT SON. Detail: structure and figures at the left.

## Plate 141

MIRACLE OF THE PENITENT SON. Detail: the structure at the right.

## Plate 142

MIRACLE OF THE MISER'S HEART. Detail: figures at the right.

## Plate 143

PIETÀ. *Bronze relief, plaquette 55 × 58.* This relief was one of those added to the altarpiece after the "general tryout" of June 13, 1448. The records (*Quaderni dell'Arca*) show that on June 23, 1449, Donatello was paid "50 lire for the metal used in modeling the *Pietà* and 113 lire for having cast and ornamented the same *Pietà*." This work was mostly executed by Donatello, but some help is noticeable in the two *Weeping Angels* on either side of the Redeemer.

## Plate 144a

SYMBOLS OF THE EVANGELISTS: *St Matthew. The first of four bronze square reliefs, 59 × 59.* In this work the master was assisted by his pupils, Giovanni da Pisa, Antonio di Chelino, Urbano da Cortona and Francesco del Valente. The *Symbols* are mentioned in documents dated from April to June 1447, which must therefore be the period of their execution. See also plates 144b and 145a and b.

## Plate 144b

SYMBOLS OF THE EVANGELISTS: *St John.*

## Color Plate III

MARY MAGDALEN. Detail of plate 162.

## Plate 145a

SYMBOLS OF THE EVANGELISTS: *St Mark.*

## Plate 145b

SYMBOLS OF THE EVANGELISTS: *St Luke.*

## Plates 146–148

SINGING AND MUSICIAN ANGELS. *Twelve rectangular bronze plaquettes, each 58 × 21.* They must originally have been placed either along the pillars of the altarpiece's frame (Kauffmann) or, more probably, along the step just below the statues, as Janson thought and now also Fiocco and P. Antonio Sartori. Sartori bases his theory on a document of March 12, 1454, which does not seem very clear to us. Ten figures of *Musician Angels* were cast in bronze in April, 1447. In June, 1447, Francesco del Valente, Giovanni da Pisa, Antonio di Chelino, Urbano da Cortona and Nicolò Pizzolo were each engaged, among other things, in preparing one angel. These works represent, therefore, a documented and direct instance of teamwork in Donatello's Paduan workshop. The master, however, must have provided designs for these *Angels*.

## Plate 149

THE DEPOSITION. *Stone relief, 139 × 188.* This work, and four other marble reliefs, were added to the Altar after the general tryout of June 13, 1448. The *Quaderni dell'Arca* show that Donatello was paid 500 *lire* for "five large stones, engraved with figures and representing the entombment of Our Lord." The *Deposition* is unquestionably one of the master's greatest plastic creations in terms of dramatic expression, and was to be carefully studied by Mantegna and Ercole de' Roberti. The plate shows a general view.

## Plate 150

TWO DOCTORS OF THE CHURCH. *Stone fragments of half-length figures standing above a parapet between two ribbed pillars, measuring, respectively, 200×31 and 187×30. Florence, Museo di Santo Spirito, from the Salvatore Romano Foundation.* The statues came from the destroyed Church of San Bartolomeo at Padua, where they were being used as steps after a sixteenth-century reconstruction. Their condition is extremely poor. Fiocco (1932) assumed that the two reliefs stood originally above the rear of Donatello's altar, at the right and left of the *Deposition.* The figures, in Fiocco's opinion, are Donatello's and represent SS Prosdocimus and Maximus. Janson (1957) rejects the theory that they could have been part of the altar, in view of the difference between their measurements and those of the figures in the *Deposition,* and refuses to list them as works executed by the master. In this we agree with Janson. Fiocco, who in his recent reconstruction of 1961, envisages the statues standing above one of the sides of the altar, as a pendant to another two *Doctors of the Church,* now lost, on the opposite side. This version would be consistent with Michiel's description of ". . . two more figures at the right and two at the left, in marble and by the hand of Donatello. . . ." The fragments could also have been included among the "five large stones, engraved with figures" mentioned in the document of April 16, 1449.

---

Plate 151

GATTAMELATA MONUMENT. *Equestrian group in bronze (about 340×390), on a masonry socle (780× 410) with two marble reliefs (120×175) by Donatello's school (now replaced by two copies). Padua, Piazza del Santo opposite the Basilica of Sant'Antonio.* We may reasonably assume that this work was begun in 1446. The last payments, relating to the stone pedestal, were recorded on May 16, 1447. Between March 10 and May 20, 1447, Donatello received more money for the casting in bronze of the horse and horseman and for removing these parts from his home. The chiseling, cleaning and chasing operations probably lasted throughout 1450. We know that litigation between Donatello and Antonio dei Narni concerning these payments was not settled until 1453, when the monument was finally erected, as we see it today, upon its pedestal, signed: OPUS DONATELLI FLO. The monument to Erasmo de Narni, called Gattamelata, was mentioned in several early epitaphs about the *Condottiere's* tomb. We find references to it in Giantonio Porcello de' Pandoni (1443–1452), Ciriaco d' Ancona (1448–1449) and Francesco Barbaro (1443–1454). Others who have mentioned this work are Bartolomeo Facio, Michele Savonarola, Filarete, Marin Sanudo, Michiel, Gelli, Vasari, Scardeone, etc. The documents were first published by A. Gloria and later by C. Boito (1897). For the decision of the Venetian Senate to erect a monument to Gattamelata (as claimed by contemporary sources but not confirmed by any official document) and the original destination of the statue, see G. Soranzo's "Due note intorno alla donatelliana statua equestre del Gattamelata," in *Bollettino del Museo Civico di Padova,* XLVI–XLVII (1957–58), pp. 21–50. The plate shows a general view, including the pedestal. See also plates 152–159.

## Plate 152

GATTAMELATA MONUMENT. Right profile of the group.

## Plate 153

GATTAMELATA MONUMENT. Left profile of the group.

## Plate 154

GATTAMELATA MONUMENT. A three-quarter photograph of the group as seen from below, against the background of the Basilica Sant'Antonio.

## Plate 155

GATTAMELATA MONUMENT. Detail: the *Condottiere*'s head.

## Plate 156

GATTAMELATA MONUMENT. Detail: the *Condottiere*'s head.

## Plate 157

GATTAMELATA MONUMENT. Detail: the horse's head.

## Plate 158

GATTAMELATA MONUMENT. Detail: the armor.

## Plates 159a and b

GATTAMELATA MONUMENT. Reliefs at the left and right of the socle.

## Plate 160

ST JOHN THE BAPTIST. *Bronze statuette; height 84.* Formerly in Berlin. *Staatliches Museen.* Probably destroyed in 1945, when the anti-aircraft tower at Friedrichshafen was set on fire. This was not the statue designed for the façade of Orvieto Cathedral, as believed by Bode (1884) and other scholars. As correctly established by Planiscig (1930), this is a late Donatello, for it embodies the harsher representation of asceticism peculiar to later works such as the *Frari Baptist* (plate 161a), the Faenza *St Jerome* (plate 161b) and others. The statuette should therefore be dated about 1450. Janson has recently taken this work from his list of Donatello's autograph sculptures and ascribed it to a Sienese master of about 1470, related to Vecchietta. This *Baptist*, however, does not reflect a Sienese interpretation of Donatello's manner (such as one may find in Vecchietta, Francesco di Giorgio, Neroccio, etc.). On the contrary the statuette seems consistent with his Paduan works, which tended to inspire, not the Sienese, but such painters of Ferrara as Ercole de' Roberti. The Berlin statuette was purchased in 1878 in Florence and was formerly in the Strozzi Palace.

## Color Plate IV

JUDITH AND HOLOFERNES. Detail of plate 166.

## Plate 161a

ST JOHN THE BAPTIST. *Statue in painted wood, 141 × 42. Venice, Church of Santa Maria dei Frari.* The statue was painted over again in the nineteenth century, and the signature, which is falsified, was probably also added or retraced in that period. It cannot be ruled out that Donatello signed this work, for many believed that he carved it in or about 1451 for the Florentine Congregation in Venice to make amends for an altar which he had failed to execute for the Frari (see "Biographical Notes"). This work is mentioned by Vasari but not directly recorded in documents. Janson believes, however, that Donatello sculptured the statue at a later date, between 1452 and 1453, that is to say, between the *Entombment* on the Santo altar and *Mary Magdalen* in the Baptistery in Florence (plate 162).

## Plate 161b

ST JEROME. *Statue in polychrome wood, 137 × 37. Faenza, Museo Civico.* Executed in or about 1452. Vasari mentions this work at the same time as another sculpture of *St John*— "In the city of Faenza he carved a wooden *St John* and *St Jerome*, which were thought to be no less admirable than his previous works." In this connection Milanesi observes: "In the convent of the Padri Riformatori in Faenza there is, however, a figure of *St Jerome* which was restored and repainted in 1845, for it was badly worm-eaten." In 1940–41, the statue was finally stripped of its nineteenth-century overlays. One should add that the critics are not unanimous in attributing this *St Jerome* to Donatello. The question is fully explored by Kauffmann (1935) and Janson. Janson finds the statue incompatible with Donatello's style around 1450. He is particularly hesitant about the pathetic expression on the saint's face. We feel, on the contrary, that the high quality of this work is fully consistent with the master's manner at the time of the *Frari Baptist* (plate 161a) and of *Mary Magdalen* (plates 162–163). St Jerome's facial expression seems to anticipate Holofernes' in the *Judith* group in the Piazza della Signoria in Florence (plates 166–172). An improbable though certainly interesting theory is that of G. Bazin (*Arts*, NO. 695, Nov. 5–11, 1958) who ascribes the Faenza *St Jerome* to the Spanish sculptor Alonso Berruguete.

## Plates 162a and b

MARY MAGDALEN. *Wooden statue, height 188. Florence, Baptistery.* This work was executed by Donatello in 1453–55, but no direct documents are available in connection with it. The sculpture is mentioned, however, by Albertini (1510), Gelli (about 1550) and Vasari (1500 and 1568). The latter in fact praised the statue's significance and value as a work of art: "It is well made, consumed with fasting and abstinence, and anatomically perfect in all its parts." The original tinting is probably concealed under a thick brown patina of incrustations. The figure is stylistically consistent with the Frari *Baptist* and the Faenza *Jerome*. The plate shows the statue as seen from the front and in profile. See also plate 163.

## Plate 163

MARY MAGDALEN. Detail of the figure's bust.

## Plates 164a and b

ST JOHN THE BAPTIST (SAN GIOVANNINO MARTELLI). *Marble statue, height 173. Florence, Bargello.* The statue represents the saint as an adolescent. He is standing and seemingly addressing an audience. His limbs are as yet delicate and unformed; his face betrays an ecstatic rapture stressed by the half-open mouth and the "seer's" eyes. The modeling of this work shows a refined technique in the surface treatment and the deep pictorial feeling. Certainly the design and probably the greater part of the execution are to be credited to the master. It is however an indisputable fact that this *Young St John* represents the "moment of maximum attraction for the taste of Desiderio" (Buscaroli). Lányi and Planiscig indeed went so far as to ascribe the statue to Desiderio. We agree with Janson (1957) that this work should definitely be restored to Donatello, but in our view he executed it after his return from Padua, that is, in or about 1455. This would appear to be confirmed by the pathetic and dramatic character of the figure which closely recalls the Baptistery's *Mary Magdalen* in Florence (plates 162–163). In general the experts who support the attribution to Donatello also favor a date between 1430 and 1435. When all is said the fact remains that the *sfumato* quality of the marble surface is typical of Desiderio. It is highly probable that Donatello left the statue unfinished and that it was later completed by another sculptor, perhaps Desiderio himself, or Antonio Rossellino. The plate shows a profile and a front view of the whole statue. See also plate 165.

## Plate 165

ST JOHN THE BAPTIST. Detail: the face.

## Plates 166a and b

JUDITH AND HOLOFERNES. *Bronze group for a fountain, on a socle with three bas-reliefs representing bacchic revelries. Height of the bronze group 236; height of the socle 55. Florence, Piazza della Signoria.* The commission for this work was probably given to Donatello by his friend Cosimo de' Medici after the sculptor's return to Florence; the group was therefore possibly executed during Donatello's last period, between 1455 and 1460. It stood originally at the top of a fountain in the gardens adjoining the Medici Palace, and was removed from that position by order of the Signoria on December 21, 1495, after the expulsion of Piero de' Medici. Later, from the side of the portal of the Town Hall of Florence, called the Palazzo Vecchio, the *Judith* group was moved to make room for Michelangelo's *David*. It stood first inside a niche in the courtyard, then, in 1506, it was installed under an arch of the Loggia della Signoria. Later still the group was removed to another arch of the same Loggia, where it stood until the First World War. Finally, in 1916, it was brought back to its original position in front of the Palazzo Vecchio.

This bronze masterpiece was formerly complicated by contrasts of colors and lights due to the marble of the socle and the bronze of the statues, which were also gilded in parts (Holofernes' belt, Judith's sword, the *putti* on Judith's breastplate, etc.). The cushion bears the inscription OPUS DONATELLI FLO. Bruno Bearzi has ascertained that the *Judith* group cast by Donatello consisted of eleven parts. The plate shows two full views of the group. See also plates 167–173 and color plate.

## Plates 167a and b

JUDITH AND HOLOFERNES. Two full views.

## Plate 168

JUDITH AND HOLOFERNES. Detail: Judith's bust.

## Color Plate IV

JUDITH AND HOLOFERNES. Detail: Judith's head.

## Plate 169

JUDITH AND HOLOFERNES. Detail: Judith's face.

## Plate 170

JUDITH AND HOLOFERNES. Detail: Judith's breastplate.

## Plate 171a

JUDITH AND HOLOFERNES. Detail: Judith's left hand.

## Plate 171b

JUDITH AND HOLOFERNES. Detail: Judith's left foot and Holofernes' right hand.

## Plate 172

JUDITH AND HOLOFERNES. Detail: Holofernes' head and bust.

## Plate 173a

JUDITH AND HOLOFERNES. First bas-relief on the socle: *Harvesting Putti*.

## Plate 173b

JUDITH AND HOLOFERNES. Second bas-relief on the socle: *Putti with a Statue of Bacchus*.

## Plate 173c

JUDITH AND HOLOFERNES. Third bas-relief on the socle: *Putti Pressing Grapes*.

## Plate 174

ST JOHN THE BAPTIST. *Bronze statue, 185 × 51. Siena, Duomo.* Having returned to Florence without finishing the two cathedral doors, Donato modeled this *Baptist* in or about 1457. By describing it as a figure "lacking its right arm," Vasari helped to spread the popular belief that Donatello had done this deliberately because he was not satisfied with the payment received. The real facts tell quite a different story. This *Baptist* was cast in three parts; when the master sent them to Siena, one arrived broken: "an arm is lacking." The statue was still lying dismembered in a storage room of the Opera del Duomo in 1467. Vasari saw the *Baptist* without its right arm which, however, was not lost. The full figure can still be admired today. The plate shows a full view of the statue. See also plates 175–176.

## Plate 175

ST JOHN THE BAPTIST. Detail: the head.

## Plate 176

ST JOHN THE BAPTIST. Detail: the left hand.

## Plate 177

HEAD OF A MAN. *Bronze, height about 38. Florence, Bargello.* There are no documents supporting the attribution, but this work must unreservedly be ascribed to Donatello's last period—between 1460 and 1465. Not only does the pathetic intensity of the facial expression proclaim the master's name, but the lineaments of the modeling, rich and yet essential in every part, are perfectly consistent with the sculptor's autograph faces in the San Lorenzo bronze *Pulpits*. This seems to be particularly true in the case of the *Descent from the Cross* (plates 185–189). If this head belongs to Donatello's late period, it cannot be related to a document of 1439 concerning a number of heads in the *Cantoria* (and discussed by Corwegh; see commentary to plate 74 and plate 82). On the strength of this document Lányi (1939) classified this *Head of a Man* among Donatello's basic works. Planiscig (1947) raised some valid objections to Lányi's theory. The first to assign the Bargello head to Donato was Bode (1900). Janson relates the whole story of this work's attributions, refuses to accept it as an autograph Donatello and ascribes it to a sculptor from Bertoldo's circle.

# THE SAN LORENZO PULPITS

The two *Pulpits* include eleven bronze reliefs. Measurements of the first *Pulpit*, situated north, at the left of the apse: *137 × 280*; measurements of the second *Pulpit*, situated south, at the right: *123 × 292*. *Florence, Church of San Lorenzo.* The north *Pulpit* is decorated with five bas-reliefs: *The Agony in the Garden; Christ before Caiaphas* and *Christ before Pilate; Crucifixion; The Descent from the Cross; The Deposition.* On the south *Pulpit* are six reliefs: *Three Women at the Tomb; The Descent into Limbo; The Resurrection; The Ascension; Pentecost* and *The Martyrdom of St Lawrence.* Other wood reliefs were added in the seventeenth century to complete the balustrade of both *Pulpits.* These carvings represented, in the north *Pulpit, The Flagellation* and *St John the Evangelist*; in the south *Pulpit, The Mocking of Christ* and *St Luke.* The commission for these two *Pulpits* was probably given to Donatello and his assistants—among whom were Bertoldo di Giovanni and Bartolomeo Bellano—by Cosimo de' Medici. The execution lasted from *c.* 1461 until Donatello's death, when work had to be interrupted.

Previtali (1961) thinks that work did not begin until about 1463. The south *Pulpit* is inscribed OPUS DONATELLI FLO (see plate 200b). For more information on the temporary and permanent installation of the two *Pulpits* inside the Basilica, and the discrimination between the reliefs executed by Donatello and those ascribed to his assistants, see pages 38–41 in "Life and Work." The *Pulpits* are the subject of an essay by M. Semrau: *Donatellos Kanzeln in San Lorenzo* (Breslau, 1891).

One might also recall that Vespasiano da Bisticci, about 1485, reported in his *Vita di Cosimo il Vecchio*, that Donatello was helped, at the time, by four "garzoni." We cannot tell if Bertoldo and Bartolomeo were included in the four.

The *Pulpits* have also been mentioned by Albertini (1510), Baccio Bandinelli (1547), Bocchi (1591) and others. In addition to the book by Semrau we again advise reading Janson's *The Sculpture of Donatello* (1957, vol. II, pp. 209–218) and Previtali's recent essay (1961). In the opinion of Laving (1959) Donatello, in choosing the rectangular shape of his *Pulpits* and the christological themes, went back to the Tuscan-Romanesque tradition but, where the proportions and some structural and compositional characteristics are concerned, was possibly inspired by classical and fourteenth-century *sarcophagi.*

Laving's paper is of interest also with regard to the funereal symbolism in Donato's pulpits: their original function was probably for the reading of lessons rather than for preaching. The theory appears feasible if one considers the original location of the *Pulpits* inside the church. In connection with the iconography of the single reliefs, Laving believes that Donatello departed deliberately from the traditional representations to which the Florentines had become accustomed in the first half of the Quattrocento, and chose to revive a number of obsolete themes and designs of the previous century, to which he added a few details and compositional solutions derived from ancient works of art.

Plate 178

NORTH PULPIT. General view. See details on plates 180–191.

Plate 179

SOUTH PULPIT. General view. See details on plates 192–200.

Plates 180a, b and c

NORTH PULPIT. Details: upper frieze.

Plate 181

NORTH PULPIT. *The Agony in the Garden*. Bas-relief on the back face. Previtali thinks that Donatello modeled this scene in wax and was probably responsible for the casting as well, though he left the cleaning, perhaps, to Bellano.

Plate 182

NORTH PULPIT. *Christ before Caiaphas*. First half of the bas-relief on the left side panel. In Previtali's opinion Donatello was responsible for casting this and the following scene, as both are parts of the same relief. The cleaning was possibly left to Bellano.

Plate 183

NORTH PULPIT. *Christ before Pilate*. Second half of the bas-relief on the left side panel.

Plate 184

NORTH PULPIT. *Crucifixion*. First relief on the front of the pulpit. Previtali claims that this scene was executed in its entirety by the master's assistants, who did not even have a wax model, though they might have benefited from a sketch or from previous works by Donatello. The modeling shows signs of Bellani and Bertoldo.

Plate 185

NORTH PULPIT. *The Descent from the Cross*. Second bas-relief on the front of the pulpit. See details on plates 186–189. Assuming that this and the following scene of *The Deposition* (plate 190) were cast by Donatello, the finishing seems to have been done by Bertoldo who, in Previtali's opinion, completed the second scene without being supervised by the master and perhaps even after the latter's death. We reject Laving's theory that the nude horsemen in the background were the result of a clumsy interference by an assistant. Laving observes, however, that these horses and riders are strikingly similar to those on the Parthenon frieze. It is a fact that Ciriaco d'Ancona did some drawings of the frieze on the spot.

Plate 186

NORTH PULPIT. *The Descent from the Cross*. Detail: the center.

Plate 187

NORTH PULPIT. *The Descent from the Cross*. Detail: the right side.

Plate 188

NORTH PULPIT. *The Descent from the Cross*. Detail: the background at the left.

Plate 189

NORTH PULPIT. *The Descent from the Cross*. Detail: the foreground at the left.

Plate 190

NORTH PULPIT. *The Deposition*. Bas-relief on the right side panel. See detail on plate 191.

Plate 191

NORTH PULPIT. *The Deposition*. Detail: the center.

## Plate 192

SOUTH PULPIT. *Three Women at the Tomb*. Bas-relief on the left side panel. There is a contrast here, noticed by Previtali, between the brilliant scheme and some feebleness in several details. Previtali thinks that this may be due to a second casting of this work, done entirely by Donatello's assistants, possibly because the master's original casting had been unsuccessful.

## Plate 193

SOUTH PULPIT. *The Descent into Limbo*. First of three bas-reliefs on the front of the pulpit. In Previtali's opinion this scene and *The Resurrection* (plate 194) were polished by the refined hand of Bertoldo, but under Donatello's strict supervision.

## Plate 194

SOUTH PULPIT. *The Resurrection*. Second relief on the front of the pulpit. See also plate 198.

## Plate 195

SOUTH PULPIT. *The Ascension*. Third relief on the front of the pulpit. Previtali believes that this relief, and especially the following one, the *Pentecost* (plate 196), were polished by Bellano, probably after Donatello's death, or at least not under his constant supervision.

## Plate 196

SOUTH PULPIT. *Pentecost*. Bas-relief on the right side panel.

## Plate 197

SOUTH PULPIT. *The Martyrdom of St Lawrence*. Bas-relief on the rear of the pulpit. At the left, carved with a burin, Previtali has spotted the date 1465 A.D.I. 16.GUG, (June 16, 1465). This should mean that Donatello finished the relief on that day. Assuming that the execution of the pulpits began in or about 1463, Previtali thinks that *The Martyrdom of St Lawrence* was the first of the cycle, and that Donatello was also responsible for the polishing. This would be an important element in establishing at what point Donatello considered a relief to have been properly finished, and a useful index in separating the master's own work from his assistants' in the execution of the other reliefs. See also plate 199.

## Plate 198

SOUTH PULPIT. *The Resurrection*. Detail: the *Risen Christ*.

## Plate 199

SOUTH PULPIT. *The Martyrdom of St Lawrence*. Detail: the first figure on the left.

## Plates 200a and b

SOUTH PULPIT. Detail: the frieze with Donatello's signature.

# LOST SCULPTURE

1. THE PROPHET DANIEL. *Florence, Duomo.* Vasari says that, during his youth, Donatello had executed "one Daniel the Prophet," in marble, for the facade of Santa Maria del Fiore. This statue has been lost, or else his should be identified with the *Isaiah* by Nanni di Banco.

2. JOSHUA. *Florence, Duomo.* This was a colossal statue in terracotta, mentioned in documents between August 27, 1410 and August 12, 1412, and designed for one of the buttresses of the tribunes in Florence Cathedral. Janson thinks it was finished not later than the summer of 1410 (Poggi, doc. 414) and was immediately placed upon the cathedral's buttress to replace Nanni di Banco's *Isaiah*, which was considered to be too small. Vasari writes that Donatello "executed for Santa Maria del Fiore two *Colossi* in cement and stucco which are placed outside the church at the corners of the chapels which they adorn." We do not know how or when these two works were lost.

3. MARBLE STATUE COATED WITH LEAD. *Florence, Duomo.* In 1415, Donatello and Brunelleschi received the commission for a marble statue, coated with gilded lead, intended for one of the cathedral's buttresses. On January 29, 1416, the metal parts were as yet uncast: Brunelleschi was peremptorily instructed to hand over to Donatello the necessary lead within seven days, and warned that if he failed to do this he would be arrested and would remain in

custody until the Opera del Duomo ordered his release.

4. ST JOHN THE BAPTIST. *Orvieto, Duomo.* Vasari states that the supervisors of the building of the Duomo in Orvieto, in a decree of February 10, 1423, authorized their chairman to give Donatello the commission for "a figure of St John the Baptist to be cast in brass, that is to say in gilded copper, for the Baptismal Font." This work should not be identified, as some have attempted to do, with the bronze version of the same subject in Berlin Museum, which was executed much later.

5. "LA DOVIZIA". *Formerly in the Old Market in Florence.* This is a stone statue, formerly located on a column in the Mercato Vecchio. Vasari reports: "In the Old Market, upon a granite column, stands a *Dovizia* by Donatello, sculptured from a rock; it is entirely isolated and so finely executed that all the experts have praised it to the utmost." In a popular poem of Donatello's time, which constitutes, in this case, a reliable if indirect document, *La Rappresentazione di Nabucodonosor, Re di Babilonia*, Donatello is asked if he is prepared to sculpture the features of the king. He answers: "I must execute the Prato *Pulpit* and now I must sculpture the *Dovizia* for the Market." In this case Donatello probably executed this statue, the first of his works completely free from any architectural setting and obviously inspired by classical art, while he was working on the Prato

*Pulpit*, that is to say, between 1428 and 1436. The *Dovizia* was ruined by time and weather, and then lost, to be replaced in 1721 by another sculpture of the same name by G. B. Foggini. A description of Donatello's *Dovizia* comes to us from Leopoldo del Migliore (*Firenze città nobilissima illustrata*, Florence, 1684). The figure had the appearance of a Goddess of Plenty, with a basket of fruit upon her head and a cornucopia supported by her right arm. A Florentine painting of the second half of the sixteenth century, reproduced by Kauffmann, shows the Mercato Vecchio with Donatello's *Dovizia* on the left. The painting, from its style, could be by Poccetti. Furthermore, a work in glass and terracotta, of the Della Robbia School, in the Buonarroti house, is definitely inspired by the master's *Dovizia*.

6. ANCIENT STATUE OF A MARSYAS, RESTORED. *Florence, formerly in the Medici Palace.* Vasari mentions the "restoration of a Marsyas," for the Medici family, carried out by Donatello. This statue in white marble and another *Marsyas* in red marble ("lo gnudo rosso"), restored by Verrocchio, stood above the portal of the Medici Palace looking out on the Via de' Ginori. When the Medici were expelled from Florence, the two statues were brought inside the Palazzo Vecchio, by order of the Signoria. Later, however, they were returned to their original position, and described by the jurist Hans Fichard of Frankfurt in 1513. After some time both works were lost.

7. ANCIENT HEADS RESTORED. *Florence.* Vasari claims that Donatello restored "an infinite number of ancient heads." These have not yet been identified.

8. GRANITE VASE. *Florence.* Vasari recalls that Donatello "sculptured in granite a beautiful vase which spouted water."

9. VASE. *Florence, formerly in the Casa Pazzi.* Vasari also recalls a vase "in the garden of the Casa Pazzi."

10. BRONZE HEAD OF THE WIFE OF COSIMO DE' MEDICI. *Florence, formerly in the Medici House.* Seen by Vasari in the duke's chambers.

11. BAS-RELIEF OF A MADONNA AND CHILD. *Florence, formerly in the Medici House.* Vasari described a relief seen by him in the chambers of the Duke of Florence and believed to be by Donatello: "A figure of Our Lady with the Child in Her arms," in *schiacciato* and adorned with illuminated *Stories* by Fra Bartolommeo. This work has not been otherwise identified.

12. BRONZE CRUCIFIX. *Florence, formerly in the Medici House.* Vasari relates that the Duke of Florence kept in his study "a beautiful, indeed miraculous Crucifix, by the hand of Donatello." This was probably a bronze crucifix of comparatively small size.

13. THE PASSION OF CHRIST. *Florence, formerly in the Medici House.* In the chambers of the Duke of Florence there was a bronze relief by Donatello representing "the Passion of Our Lord, with a great number of figures." This work is either lost or not identifiable.

14. BAS-RELIEF OF A CRUCIFIXION IN BRONZE. *Florence, formerly in the Medici House.* This relief, seen by Vasari in the Duke's chambers, cannot be identified with any degree of certainty. Perhaps it

was the *Crucifixion* in the Bargello (plate 210a), designed by Donatello but executed by his workshop or school and not mentioned in documents.

15. VIRGIN AND CHILD. *Florence, formerly the property of the heirs of Jacopo Capponi.* This was a marble half-relief, which Vasari described as "considered to be an extremely rare object," in the house of the heirs of Jacopo Capponi. The relief has not been identified.

16. RELIEF OF A HALF-LENGTH FIGURE OF A MADONNA. *Florence, formerly the property of Giulio de' Nobili.* This work, which is either lost or not otherwise identifiable, was thus described by Vasari: "Master Antonia de' Nobili, who was a depositary of His Excellency, had in his house a marble picture by the hand of Donato representing in bas-relief a half-length figure of Our Lady."

17. MADONNA AND CHILD. *Florence, formerly the property of Bartolomeo Gondi.* This is another lost or unidentified "half-relief," recalled by Vasari: "The Madonna and Child sculptured by Donatello with such love and diligence that one cannot see a more beautiful thing, nor imagine how Donatello could have been so spontaneous in modeling the Virgin's hair and her beautiful drapery." This description by Vasari leads us to suspect that he may have seen a relief in Agostino Duccio's manner.

18. MADONNA. *Florence.* Formerly the property of Messer Lelio Torelli. This work is also described by Vasari as "by the hand of the same Donatello."

19. MARBLE HEAD. *Urbino, formerly the property of Duke Guidobaldo da Montefeltro.* This "beautiful head of marble" thought to be by Donatello, in the chambers of the Duke of Urbino, is also recalled by Vasari.

20. HERALDIC ARMS. *Florence, formerly the property of the Da Sommaia family.* Donatello, Vasari says, was considered responsible for many coats-of-arms of Florentine noble families among which was "a beautiful escutcheon in the home of the Sommaja," that is to say, the Da Sommaia.

21. FIVE MARBLE BAS-RELIEFS INCLUDING AN "ETERNAL FATHER." *Padua, previously on the rear of the Altar of the Saint, Basilica of St Anthony.* After the tryout of June 13, 1448, Donatello, as we know, added to the altarpiece an *Entombment* in stone, which still exists, and five other marble reliefs, among them the *Eternal Father*. All these have been lost. We do not know the theme of the other four reliefs. All five works are simply described as "five great stones sculptured with figures, including the *Entombment of Our Lord*." In connection with the identification of these two reliefs, suggested by Fiocco, see commentary to plate 150.

22. THREE STATUES OF THE VIRGIN. *Formerly in Mantua.* These are three sculptures executed by Donatello between 1450 and 1451, which he sent to Marchese Ludovico Gonzaga in Mantua. One of the statues was in plaster, the other two in terracotta.

23. PLASTER STATUE OF ST ANDREW. *Formerly in Mantua.* A small wax bas-relief, arranged on a

wooden board, executed between 1450 and 1451, and sent to Marchese Ludovico Gonzaga.

24. THREE RIBBED COLUMNS, WITH PEDESTALS AND CAPITALS. Formerly at Mantua and, as in the case of the previous work, sent by Donatello to Ludovico Gonzaga.

25. WOODEN MODEL, COATED WITH WAX, FOR AN ALTAR. *Formerly in Venice, Church of the Frari.* We know that Donatello executed this model for an altar intended for a chapel (probably for the Florentines residing in Venice) in the Frari Church. The altar, which was never executed, was later compensated for by Donatello's *St John the Baptist.*

26. MADONNA AND CHILD WITH TWO ANGELS. *Formerly the property of Giovanni Chellini (1373–1462).* This work is recalled in a passage from the "Discorso di Scipione Ammirati sopra la famiglia de' Samminiati" (Florence, National Library, Passerini manuscript, 191,

NO. 38); it reads as follows: "He (G. Chellini) became friendly with that most famous of sculptors Donatello, whom, thanks to divine assistance, he healed of his infirmity. Donato then gave him a *Tondo* as large as a platter upon which he had done a Virgin Mary with the Child in her arms and one angel on each side. This work was all in bronze and carved on one side so that one could throw upon it molten glass and reproduce the same figure from that side of the *Tondo.* This happened in the year 1456."

27. WAX MODEL FOR THE PORTALS OF THE CATHEDRAL. *Formerly in Siena.* In 1457, Donatello executed in Siena the wax models for the Duomo portals. This work was never cast in bronze. These waxen models, now lost, are recorded as follows in two inventories of 1467 and 1480: "Two designs for the Cathedral door sculptured by Donatello, with figures of wax" . . . "Two designs for the Duomo portals by Donatello with figures. . . ."

# SCULPTURE ATTRIBUTED TO DONATELLO

The sculptures ascribed to Donatello constitute a true and proper corpus which includes, of course, the extensive and complex problem of reconstructing the activities and personalities of his many assistants, collaborators and followers, more or less directly connected with the master. There are, on the other hand, several questions concerning works, in Donatello's manner, of extremely high quality. These the modern critics have often eliminated from the list of works considered worthy of Donatello. In this section the attributions which have been definitely superseded will not be mentioned.

## Plate 201

FIGURE OF PROPHET. *Marble, height 85. Paris, Musée Jacquemart-André.* Keeping in mind the diversity in style between the two *Profetini* above the Porta della Mandorla in the Duomo in Florence (plates 1 and 2), traditionally ascribed to Donatello, Valentiner assigns to Donatello the *Prophet* on the right (now generally attributed to Nanni di Banco), but rejects the attribution in the case of the *Prophet* on the left which he considers to have been executed by a minor artist, probably Jacopo di Piero Guidi. Valentiner, however, publishes this *Prophet* in the Jacquemart-André as a work by Donatello, and he assumes it was the original pendant to the one on the right above the Porta della Mandorla. Valentiner says this work was re-placed by the *First Prophet*, which he also assigns to a transitory artist, some time later. In the first place, the measurements of the *Profetino* at the right do not correspond to those of the sculpture above the door. (The latter figure is taller, being 123 high.) In the second place, the representation of the two statues is not consonant. Because Vaccarino stressed the difference in size (1951 and 1959), Valentiner altered his line of reasoning. The Jacquemart-André statuette, he said then, can be identified with Donatello's *Prophet* as mentioned in the document of 1408. Since it was smaller than the other figure above the Porta della Mandorla, it would now appear that Donatello was asked to execute two more statues of prophets in a larger size. Of these he seems to have sculptured only the one on the right; the figure on the left—probably an *Announcing Angel*, by Jacopo di Piero—was, we learn, used only provisionally to make good Donatello's failure to carry out the whole of his commission. Besides finding this interpretation of an incomplete document far too hypothetical, we note that the flat folds of geometrical shape in the robes of the Jacquemart-André statuette reveal an earlier experiment in *schiacciato* technique. Such a technique does not figure before 1425–30 in Donatello's work. We are, therefore, confronted with a sculpture executed much later than 1408, when the master did the

*Profetini* on the Mandorla door. In our view the anonymous artist was one of Donatello's first direct followers.

## Plate 202

BUST OF A WOMAN (called St Cecilia). *Terracotta bust, height 46. London, Victoria and Albert Museum. From the Gigli-Campana Collection.* Some critics have been fairly definite in doubting the authenticity of this work (Meyer, Schottmüller, Venturi, Cruttwell, etc.), without, however, referring to the strictly non-Donatellesque character of the artistry. In favor of the attribution of this bust to Donatello are Maclagan and Longhurst, who believed it to have been executed in or about 1440. While we find no reason to doubt the authenticity of this bust—in spite of the decayed patina it still reveals a very high lyrical quality—we submit that the sculptor was not Donatello but Michelozzo. If one compares this work with the *Angels* which were formerly part of the *Aragazzi Monument* (now in the Victoria and Albert Museum) and with other confirmed works by Michelozzo, the *St Cecilia* will definitely appear to be his.

## Plate 203

MADONNA AND CHILD WITH ANGELS AND SAINTS. *Oval relief in polychrome plaster, 42 × 32. Victoria and Albert Museum, London.* Probably from a bronze original. The attribution to Donatello seems very valid. A similar relief, with four angels, was formerly in the Werner Weisbach Collection in Berlin. The polychromy is original. Some real analogies have been detected between the musician angel at the left and the violin player in the background of *Herod's Feast* in the Siena Baptistery (plate 43). So far as the remainder is concerned, the representational similarities would seem to point rather in the direction of another relief of the same subject, *The Dance of Salome* in the Lille Museum (plate 71). The date of about 1430, submitted by Schottmüller, appears therefore fairly convincing. If one looks at the figure of the *Child*, sturdy enough to recall Masaccio, one cannot but agree with those critics who claim that Masaccio influenced Donatello. We know, furthermore, that Donatello met Masaccio in Pisa in 1427 when the painter was executing there his famous *Carmine Polyptych*.

## Plate 204

ST JOHN THE BAPTIST. *Marble, 170. Florence, Museo Nazionale.* This unique sculpture has puzzled and divided the experts who, however, have always tended to accept it within at least Donatello's ambience. Venturi favors Michelozzo; Schottmüller a collaboration between the two partners; Schubring, Colasanti, Buscaroli and others have firmly supported the attribution to Donatello.

The one exception is Kauffmann, who has correctly pointed out that the statue belongs in fact to the civilization of the Cinquecento. He sees in the incisive anatomical style of this work the plastic manner of Francesco da Sangallo. The problem of the attribution has recently been re-examined by Parronchi ("Il San Giovanni Battista 'Gradivo' del Bargello, opera misconosciuta di Michelangelo", in *Studi Urbinati*, XXXIV, New Series B, NOS. 1–2 (1960) 68–83). Parronchi, having examined the critical history of this interesting sculpture, has suggested that it be attributed to the young Michelangelo.

Thus Parronchi picks up Longhi's earlier theory concerning the *San Giovannino* in the Church of the Fiorentini in Rome, with which this *St John the Baptist* reveals some analogies. Parronchi's suggestion, which is undoubtedly a considered one, confirms in any case the early Cinquecento character of the Bargello statue.

Plate 205a

FLAGELLATION. *Marble relief, 46.5 × 57.5. Formerly Staatliches Museen, Berlin.* Purchased in Florence in 1892 by the Peruzzi family, this work was destroyed in 1945 by the war. Kauffmann (1935) claimed it unreservedly for Donatello, while Schottmüller (1933) was uncertain and did not think that the master could have possibly executed the whole relief. Indeed Christ's face and other strained or weak areas lead us to suspect an imitator of Donatello, although an experienced and capable one. If so he was certainly inspired, especially as to the perspective, by works which Donatello executed between 1425 and 1430, such as the two versions of the *Herod's Feast* in the Siena Baptistery (plate 42) and the *Dance of Salome* in Lille Museum (plate 71). These similarities, however, would seem to be the result of fixed artistic canons. In other words they may indicate that the anonymous and scarcely consistent imitator of Donatello elaborated upon the master's themes at a later date, possibly in the period 1440-45. Janson too, in reporting (1957) the attributions centered on this work, speaks of a "pastiche" which, in his view, was not executed before 1460-70.

Plate 205b

CHRIST IN THE SEPULCHRE.

*Marble relief, 45 × 81. London, Victoria and Albert Museum. From the Gigli-Campana Collection.* The doubts Schottmüller expressed about its authenticity (1904) do not seem valid to us. Bode, Semper, Reymond and others ascribe it to Donatello; Adolfo Venturi to the master's school. Again, the compilers of the Victoria and Albert Museum's catalogue, E. Maclagan and M. H. Longhurst (1932), attribute the relief to Donatello, and so does Kauffmann (1935). In fact this work is by a follower and collaborator of Donatello who executed it in or about 1440-45. This artist made use of the *schiacciato* technique in order to infuse into his metal a precious, decorative, but superficial quality. The relief is sadly lacking in pictorial complexity. The forms in the foreground have a plastic value that the linear development is intended to stress. This anonymous sculptor was partly influenced by Donatello's works executed in Rome and partly by the *putti* in the Prato *Pulpit* (plates 83-87). He probably assisted the master in the Prato workshop. His individuality, a fairly remarkable one, is expressed in a manner not too different from that of another Donatellesque relief in the Victoria and Albert Museum, the so-called *Madonna of the Rose*. Martinelli has recently attributed this *Christ in the Sepulchre* to Michelozzo, holding that the relief was part of the decoration of an altar which included *Delivery of the Keys* in the Victoria and Albert Museum (plate 55) and the *Tabernacle of the Sacrament* in St Peter's (plates 68-69). See the commentaries in connection with the two latter works. We do not agree with the attribution to Michelozzo, because of some chronological problems: the antecedents of *Christ*

123

*in the Sepulchre* should presumably be the *Cantoria* (plates 74–82) and the reliefs on the Prato *Pulpit* (plates 83–87), two works which it cannot have preceded in time. But the commission for the *Cantoria* was given to Donatello in 1433, and although the first contract for the Prato *Pulpit* was signed in 1429, he did not begin until the signing of a second contract in 1434. Three reliefs for the *Pulpit* were moved from Florence to Prato as late as 1436. (See "Biographical Notes".) Pope-Hennessy too (1959), rejects the attribution to Michelozzo submitted by Martinelli and considers it impossible that this relief could have been an iconographical part of the same unit as the *Tabernacle of the Sacrament*. This *Christ in the Sepulchre*, in the opinion of Pope-Hennessy, is merely a rendition of Donatello's model done, in the thirties, by the same disciple who did the greater part of the *Madonna and Child in the Clouds* in Boston (plate 57). In support of his theory, Pope-Hennessy stresses the resemblance between the angels in the London and Boston reliefs and between these and the *putti* in the first two reliefs from the left on the Prato *Pulpit*. He adds, however, that Donatello himself executed or retouched the finer and more vigorous parts, plastically speaking, of Christ's figure, such as the left arm and side of the body and especially the head. Pope-Hennessy, furthermore, would not be averse to accepting a later date of execution, perhaps the Paduan period, for this work which had obviously a remarkable influence upon Giovanni Bellini's *Pietà* in Rimini.

### Plate 206a

MADONNA AND CHILD. *Bas-relief in stucco, 78 × 64. London, Victoria and Albert Museum.* From the Gigli-Campana Collection. Surely this work presupposes the typology of the *Pazzi Madonna* (plate 38). It is attributed to the master in the catalogue by E. Maclagan and M. H. Longhurst (1932), but in our view it is a workshop product.

### Plate 206b

MADONNA. *Bas-relief in gilded terracotta, 74 × 56.5. London, Victoria and Albert Museum.* A work of a very high quality in the sensitive treatment of the *schiacciato* surface and for the nervous vitality of the sculptor's execution. It is consistent with Donatello's manner around 1440. Bode, Schubring, Maclagan, M. H. Longhurst and, recently, Pope-Hennessy (1959) have attributed it to the master. The latter critic thinks that it was sculptured after Donatello's stay in Padua. Others have doubted the authenticity of this work, but not for the right reasons. It is definitely by a collaborator of Donatello who studied not only the master's sculptures but also the works of painters such as Lippi. This is proved by the typology of the Child.

### Plate 207a

MADONNA AND CHILD. *Bas-relief in polychrome stucco, 55 × 37. Rome, private collection.* From the collection of Prince Fabrizio Massimo. The tinting has faded until it resembles a bronze patina on the surface. The attribution to Donatello is traditional. The faces touching each other are reminiscent of the *Pazzi Madonna* (plate 38), but with many variations. The intensity of the eyes and the general modeling certainly reveal a very high quality. The most reasonable assumption is that this relief was executed from a lost prototype by the master, possibly of the early Paduan period. On the other hand there are no other known replicas of this *Massimo Madonna*, which can therefore be considered as a unique example of Donatello's sculpture.

## Plate 207b

MADONNA AND CHILD WITH FOUR CHERUBS. *Bas-relief in polychrome stucco, 102 × 72. Formerly in Staatliches Museum, Berlin.* This work was unfortunately destroyed in 1945 in the war. It was purchased in 1888 in Florence and came originally from the Church of Santa Maria Maddalena de' Pazzi. The attribution to Donatello (Schottmüller, 1933) was confirmed by Kauffmann (1935), who considers the relief was executed in or about 1435, because of its analogies with the *Annunciation* in Santa Croce (plates 88–94). In this Kauffmann seems to agree with Knapp (1923) and to disagree with Schubring (1907) and Bertaux (1910), who believe the relief was finished after the Paduan period. This work reveals several formal similarities to many details of the Santa Croce *Annunciation*; on the other hand, the frequency of lines in the drapery's pleats and the rather full and peasant-like faces of the Virgin, Child and cherubs point to a late follower of Donatello, an artist who may even have studied Verrocchio, a facile sculptor who, though he could easily imitate the master's works of the period 1435–40, was equally conversant with Donatello's later experiments.

## Plate 208a

CRUCIFIXION. *Bas-relief in stucco, 36.5 × 26.5. Berlin, Staatliches Museum.* This is a roughed-out work, executed in Donatello's last dramatic manner by an anonymous sculptor. It shows a number of similarities to the De' Forzori relief in the Victoria and Albert Museum (plate 209). This *Crucifixion*, which is in very poor condition, has been attributed to the master by Bode, Colasanti and more recently by Kauffmann (1935) whose book, *Donatello* (Berlin) contains all the necessary bibliographical information.

## Plate 208b

CRUCIFIXION. *Bronze relief, 40 × 27. Paris, Louvre.* The attribution to Donatello, suggested by Bode, has been supported by Kauffmann (1953). The latter sees a very strong relationship between this work, the altar called *De' Forzori* in the Victoria and Albert Museum and the Berlin *Crucifixion* (plate 208a). We do not agree that the connection is as overwhelmingly evident as Kauffmann would have it. In the first place the Forzori altar and the Berlin *Crucifixion* are themselves works of dubious authorship; secondly this bronze relief, though admittedly a valuable sculpture and certainly inspired by the masterpieces of the late Donatello, is by a follower. Janson (1957, p. 244) finds a link between this work, the *Martyrdom of St Sebastian* in the Musée Jacquemart-André (plate 211) and a *Madonna and two Angels* in Vienna. He dates these three bronze reliefs about 1470 and attributes them to an anonymous imitator of Donatello's late style, also associated with the Medici *Crucifixion* (plate 210).

## Plate 208c

FLAGELLATION. *Bronze plaquette, 14 × 19.6. Formerly in Berlin, Staatliches Museen,* and destroyed in the war in 1945. Other replicas are in Paris and Strasbourg. The attribution of this plaquette to Donatello's post-Paduan period was recently upheld by Kauffmann (1935). In our view the execution is by an anonymous imitator.

## Plate 209

FLAGELLATION AND CRUCI-FIXION, WITH PREDELLA. *Terracotta relief roughed out for an altar, called De' Forzori, 53.5 × 57.3; predella (with putti, medallions and festoons), 11 × 57.5. London, Victoria and Albert Museum. From the Gigli-Campana Collection.* The two representations are presented within two vaulted enclosures, a fact which presumably indicates some influence derived from the reliefs in the Santo in Padua. The formal elements and the dramatic tone of these two scenes are typical of Donatello's last period, and the relief may therefore be reasonably included in the decade 1450–60. But if the inspiration is strongly Donatellesque, the same cannot be said for the quality of the execution, which is definitely below the master's standard: formal weaknesses in the dynamic structure of the images, attachments of limbs, etc., which cannot be exclusively imputed to the methods of a sculptor "roughing out" his models. Donatello's manner in this work is due purely to enthusiastic reflection, not to the direct assertion of genius. The attribution to the master is accepted by most critics: Bode, Schubring and others, the most recent being Maclagan and Longhurst. A. Venturi, for his part, submitted the name of Giovanni da Pisa. A detailed study of this terracotta was carried out by M. Semrau ("Donatello und die sogenannte Forzori Altar," in *Kunstwissenchaftliche Beitrage August Schmarsow gewidmet*, 1907). A drawing in the Uffizi, representing a *Flagellation* under a vaulted ceiling, shows some analogies with this work. The author of the drawing (in our view Nicolò Pizzolo) and of the terracotta were both inspired by Donatello's manner and should therefore be considered of his school.

## Plate 210

CRUCIFIXION. *Bronze relief gilded in parts, 43 × 70. Florence, Museo Nazionale.* In spite of the fact that no documents are available, it is reasonable to identify this relief with a *Crucifixion* mentioned by Vasari as part of the Medici treasures. Borghini also recalls a bronze panel, representing Christ upon the Cross and other figures, in the Duke's reception room. This work was attributed to Donatello by Schubring (1907), Kauffman (1935) and more recently by the *Catalogo della Mostra dei Bronzetti Italiani del Rinascimento* (1962), in which the relief is hypothetically dated about 1455. Janson, on the other hand, suggests an anonymous follower about 1470, perhaps the same artist responsible for the Louvre *Crucifixion* (plate 208b) and the *Martyrdom of St Sebastian* in the Musée Jacquemart-André (plate 211). This relief betrays, in our view, the same problematic evidence of a collaboration, with the assistants playing a dominant role, that we find in the San Lorenzo *Pulpits* (plates 178–200). Ruling out the contribution (which in our opinion cannot be positively established) of young Bertoldo (Tschudi, Planiscig, etc.), we detect in this bas-relief the hand of an unknown assistant who translated a design, or an "invention" by Donatello. The articulated and energetic style of the modeling reveals a dramatic dignity in the foreground, totally unmatched by the landscape and soldiers in the *schiacciato* background, which are merely inert instances of a declining illustrational art. A further sign of decadence, in our view, is the artist's preference for gilded margins and armor. This is, however, a Donatello *Crucifixion* and, as such, much more significant than the Paris (plate 208b) and Berlin (plate 208a) versions, and more important than certain parts of the Forzori altar in London (plate 209).

### Plate 211

MARTYRDOM OF ST SEBASTIAN. *Bronze relief, 22 × 16. Paris, Musée Jacquemart-André.* This is a large bronze plaquette generally ascribed —and rightly so—to Donatello's school. Kauffmann, however (1935), assigns it unreservedly to the master. We advise reading his book which contains important information concerning this and the previous work. Janson's opinion is stated in the commentaries to plates 208b and 210. This anonymous artist, who tends to prolong his forms, imparts an added "preciousness" to Donato's linear rhythms and pictorial modeling, which, in the master's works, achieve the intense dramatic significance we know so well.

### Plate 212

THE REDEEMER'S BLOOD. *Relief on a marble lunette, 39.8 × 67. Torrita, Maestri Hospital.* Formerly, for many years, above the entrance of the Chapel of the Madonna della Neve, adjoining the Hospital. This work was published by Bode ("A newly discovered bas-relief by Donatello," in *The Burlington Magazine* (1925), pp. 108–14) as a completely autograph sculpture by the master. However, as recently estab-

lished (1959) by Pope-Hennessy, it is only a mediocre workshop product, even though the undoubtedly original idea and some of the details could have been derived from a drawing by Donatello. Pope-Hennessy believes that this work should be dated about 1440–45, because of its obvious derivation from the *Annunciation* at Naples and close analogies with reliefs on the Prato *Pulpit*. In view of the Eucharistic theme, Pope-Hennessy also considers that the lunette may at one time have been part of a Tabernacle by Donatello, perhaps even the upper part of the *Tabernacle of the Sacrament* (plate 68): the measurements do not seem to contradict this assumption and furthermore the lateral angels in the lunette could have been modeled by the same hand that did the ones in the lower part of the *Tabernacle of the Sacrament*.

### Plate 213

LAMENTATION. *Bronze relief, 33.5 × 41.5. London, Victoria and Albert Museum.* The background of this relief seems to have been entirely cut off, perhaps because of an unsuccessful casting, from the *schiacciato* figures in motion. The violence and drama implicit in the style of this work, superficial though they may be, do recall Donatello's late manner, after the Padua experience and especially after the San Lorenzo *Pulpits* (plates 178–200). In our view, though there may be a reference here to an original sketch or roughed-out model by the master, someone else was responsible for the final work. The convulsive rhythm of the action becomes uncontrolled, as for instance, in the Virgin's figure and the deformed images. While it is true that Donatello's revolt against classicism justified such methods, the fact remains that his expressions preserved, even at their most extreme, an inner sense of "measure" which is totally absent from this work. Beginning with Semper (1887), most critics have unanimously attributed this relief to Donatello, but in reality it is the creation of an extremely gifted and direct collaborator of the master's late period. Kauffmann (1935) reiterates the attribution to Donatello, praising it and stressing its relationship to the commission (1457) for the *Bronze Doors* in Siena. Indeed Kauffmann's views have been developed further by Janson (1957). Briefly, this bas-relief of the *Lamentation* should, or could, be a bronze model for the door panels in Siena, of which two wax models are known to have existed. Last but not least, Pope-Hennessy (1959) has confirmed the attribution to Donatello, adding, however, that it was finished about 1440–43, which would closely associate this work in time with the *Bronze Doors* of the Old Sacristy of San Lorenzo.

### Plate 214a

NATIVITY. *Stucco relief, 67 × 67. London, Victoria and Albert Museum.* The scene is represented in the shape of a *tondo* inscribed within a square. St Joseph is sleeping at the right; in the center, the Child lies in the manger; the Virgin appears on the left. This work is obviously by an imitator, a man, let us hasten to add, who can narrate a story, translate it into a pleasant, formal style and mold his figures into enjoyable images, with a tendency to *schiacciato*. This artist, however, departs from the master's more direct manner, in that he visibly prefers a pictorial technique more like Lippi's and a sculptural one reminiscent of

Bernardo Rossellino. It is possibly the same man who sculptured the *Spinelli Madonna*, dated 1441, also in the Victoria and Albert Museum. His activities, because of certain analogies with the school of Squarcione, may have been carried out in the Veneto region. Maclagan and Longhurst (1932) think, however, that this relief is directly derived from a prototype by Donatello. Pope-Hennessy (1959) suggests a fairly convincing attribution to Urbano da Cortona in or about 1460, on the strength of certain facial similarities with some of the reliefs in the Chapel of the Madonna delle Grazie in Siena Cathedral (1451–55).

### Plates 214b–215f

EIGHT TONDI: DIOMEDES SEIZES THE TROJAN PALLADIUM; FAUN WITH THE CHILD DIONYSUS; CENTAUR WITH A BASKET OF FRUIT; BACCHUS AND ARIADNE; ULYSSES AND ATHENA: SCYTHIAN PRISONER BEFORE A ROMAN GENERAL; DAEDALUS AND ICARUS; TRIUMPH OF LOVE. *Marble reliefs, diameter of each tondo 98. In the courtyard of the Medici-Riccardi Palace, Florence.* These marble *tondi* are an obvious and deliberate imitation of figures from Hellenistic-Roman sarcophagi, gems and cameos. The attribution to Donatello goes back to Vasari: "In the first court of the Casa Medici there are eight marble medallions containing representations of ancient cameos, the reverse of medals and some scenes very beautifully executed by him (Donatello); these works are cemented into the frieze between the windows and the lintel, above the arches of the *loggie*." Many have doubted the validity of Vasari's attribution, which was, however, accepted by E. Kris

(1929) and by Kauffmann (1935). If these reliefs were authentic they should be assigned to Donatello's late period, because of the Medici fleur-de-lis interpolated between the *tondi*: permission to use the French royal emblem in the family's coat-of-arms was granted to Piero de' Medici by the King of France in 1465. But the sculptural style of these medallions, implying as they do a cold and even strained imitation of antique works of art, leads us to reject Donatello's authorship in favor of an anonymous follower, whom Buscaroli (1942) imagines, without much foundation, to have belonged to the Prato workshop. Buscaroli suggests Maso di Bartolomeo. See plates 214b and c and 215a–f.

### Plate 216a

MADONNA AND CHILD (VERONESE MADONNA). *Terracotta relief, 76 × 53. Florence, Museo Nazionale.* The name *Veronese* is due to the existence of a copy of this work, by no means the best one, for there are several, near the tombs of the Della Scala family in Verona.

All the existing versions of the *Veronese Madonna* betray the hand of followers or assistants of the Paduan period who have altered, transformed and certainly weakened a lost prototype by the master. Kauffmann (1935) believes that the best version is the one in polychrome stucco in the Metropolitan Museum of New York. Other copies, such as a stucco in the Victoria and Albert Museum in London and a polychrome terracotta formerly in the Von Beckerath Collection and now in the Krefeld Museum, are definitely inferior to the rest of these works. The best are undoubtedly the polychrome stucco in the Staatliches Museen in Berlin and this one in the Bargello.

### Plate 216b

MADONNA AND CHILD. *Bas-relief in polychrome stucco, 68.5 × 66. Raleigh, North Carolina Museum of Art.* This is the work of a follower who has translated Donatello's anti-classicism into an anti-literary mannerism by reviving the master's energetic plastic experiment while he was in Padua and afterwards. This artist, however, is not lacking in individuality, especially when it comes to rhythm and lines, shallow though they may be. The stucco was formerly in the Bardini Collection in Florence; later it became the property of Werner Weisbach of Berlin. The attribution to Donatello can be found in the *North Carolina Museum of Art Bulletin*, VOL. I, NO. 1 (1957).

### Plate 217a

PORTRAIT BUST OF MARCHESE LUDOVICO III GONZAGA. *Bronze bust, 36.5 × 28. Paris, Musée Jacquemart-André.* This work, and another portrait-bust in Berlin Museum which strongly resembles it, have been attributed to Donatello during his stay in Mantua in the summer of 1450. The sitter's identification with Gonzaga is due to Hermann Grimm (1883). A careful analysis of the two busts, along the lines of the study carried out by Kauffmann (1935), has led to the conclusion that the Berlin portrait is by Donatello and the one in Paris is no more than a copy.

The Jacquemart-André bust, however, is not a reproduction of the Berlin masterpiece, for it exhibits several subtle facial differences and, in our view, is more strongly characterized than the version which Kauffmann and others consider to be an original Donatello. It is our contention that both works are school products derived from a lost original by the master.

## Plate 217b

BUST OF HOMER. *Black stone, height 45. Florence, Uffizi.* Elena Berti Toesca considers, very reasonably, that this head and other similar works, that is to say, the *Euripides* in the Galleria D'Este in Modena, a bronze head in the Musée Jacquemart-André in Paris, a bust in grey stone in the Capitoline Museum in Rome, are all derived from a probably lost prototype by Donatello. That this *Homer* strongly recalls the *Pulpits* in San Lorenzo (plates 178–200) and the head of *Holofernes* (plate 172) is obvious enough. Donatello's original, if it ever existed, must have been executed between 1455 and 1465. If that is so, then we are confronted with the interesting possibility that Donatello actually imitated the ancient masters, which in turn would involve us in the complex subject of Renaissance forgeries of Greek and Roman sculptures. On the other hand we must not forget that such archeologists as Heckler and Amelung (in the case of the *Homer*) and Stuart-Jones (in connection with the head in Rome's Capitoline) have claimed these works as authentic ancient sculpture.

## Plate 218

"NICCOLÒ DA UZZANO." *Polychrome terracotta, 46×44. Florence, Museo Nazionale.* The tinting is not original, but merely the result of several successive repaintings. The theory that the figure's face was modeled after a death-mask is very convincing. The relaxed skin and muscles and the ruthless representational realism displayed here are typical of a mask; at the same time the sculptor has enlivened the head considerably. See, however, the technical comments of J. Pohl (1938).

Not all the critics agree that the sitter was Uzzano. The earliest reference available on this matter is a statement by Ferrante Capponi (1643–1714) who owned the bust and had it inscribed: MAGNO ET SPECTATO VIRO — NICOLAO DE UZANO — FERRANTES CAPPONIUS MAIORI SUO. Some modern experts have suggested other identifications, such as Pier Capponi (De Fabriczy, 1903); Gino Capponi (Bertaux, 1910); Cicero (Studniczka, 1924). The first to indicate this bust as a work by Donatello was Carlo Carlieri (*Ristretto delle cose piu notabili della città di Firenze*, fifth edition, 1745; the previous editions are not available). The attribution, which had been doubted, but only by a few, was strongly supported by Kauffmann (1935) who also accepts the identification as Uzzano. More recently, on the other hand, this terracotta was excluded from the catalogue of Donatello's works by L. Planiscig, O. Morisani and H. W. Janson, whom we recommend to readers who desire to know more details. In our opinion the Bargello Uzzano, though influenced by Donatello, was not executed by the master. The figure's face lacks the enlivening impulse and aggressive "bite" peculiar to Donatello's modeling. At the same time it reveals several realistic and technical features which prove that this anonymous imitator was familiar with Donatello's great Paduan works and had paid special attention to his late expressionism. Not, therefore, 1432 (as generally suggested for this work), but about 1460.

## Plate 219

BAPTISM OF CHRIST. *Marble relief. Arezzo Cathedral, Baptismal Font.* The surface is considerably worn in several places. Mentioned by Vasari as a work by Donatello's brother Simone and first published by F. Schottmüller ("Zur Donatello Forschung", in *Monatshefte für Kunstwissenschaft*, VOL. II (1909), 38–45). Schottmüller definitely attributed it to the master, dating it between the *St George and the Dragon* at Orsanmichele and *Delivery of the Keys* in London, that is to say, in or about 1429.

His suggestion was not accepted until 1959, when Pope-Hennessy took up the attribution, but submitted an earlier date—about 1410–12. The Arezzo relief, according to Pope-Hennessy, was the first brilliant, though still tentative, experiment by Donatello in the field of *schiacciato*. The critic found at the same time some similarities between this *Baptism* and some of Donatello's early works such as the Bargello *David*, the *St George* and the *First Prophet* of the Campanile cycle. In fact, this work is an extremely interesting and problematical sculpture, some elements of which are certainly derived from such examples of Donatello's work in the third or fourth decade of the century as *The Annunciation*, *Delivery of the Keys*, and the *Dance of Salome*. The general manner and other motifs, however, are not Donatello's; nor can we accept that the waverings, the inequalities, the technical and stylistic insufficiencies, the errors of perspective revealed by this *Baptism* can all be explained by the master's youth at the time of execution. The relief, in our opinion, is the work of an anonymous, though capable, imitator of about 1440.

Plate 220

DANCING PUTTO. *Bronze statuette, height 38.5. Florence, Museo Nazionale.* The dispute centered on this *Putto*, and whether it should or should not be attributed to Donatello, is complicated by those who relate it to the two statuettes by Donatello on the Tabernacle of the Baptismal Font in Siena (plates 43a and b). The whole question has been thoroughly investigated and elucidated by H. W. Janson, who correctly rejects the attribution to the master. In this Janson agrees with Lányi (*Burlington Magazine* [1939], 142ff.) who ascribed the statuette to an anonymous Sienese of the late Quattrocento. But the *Catalogo della Mostra dei Bronzetti Italiani del Rinascimento* (1962, NO. 3) still ascribes this work to Donatello.

Plate 221

TOMB OF ONOFRIO STROZZI. *Florence, Sacristy of Santa Trinita.* From a document of August 4, 1418, we learn that the tomb was begun by Piero di Nicolò Lamberti before that date. Lisner, however (1958), claims that Donatello received from Palla Strozzi the commission for this work, designed and executed a model for it, and probably also devised the frieze on the main arch, with *putti* and festoons, the execution being carried out by his workshop. Piero Lamberti is believed to have executed, from Donatello's model, the frieze on the rear arch and the sculptural decoration of the sarcophagus. Gosebruch (1958) attributes the project for the *Tomb of Onofrio Strozzi* to Michelozzo.

# LOCATION OF SCULPTURE

## AREZZO
### CATHEDRAL
*Baptism of Christ* (plate 219; attribution).

## BERLIN
### STAATLICHES MUSEEN
*The Pazzi Madonna* (plate 38).
*Angel with Tambourine* (plate 48c).
*David* (plate 116).
*Crucifixion* (plate 208a; attribution).
Works destroyed or lost during the last war:
*St John the Baptist* (plate 160).
*Flagellation* (plate 205a; attribution).
*Madonna and Child with Four Cherubs* (plate 207b; attribution).
*Flagellation* (plate 208c; attribution).

## BOSTON
### MUSEUM OF FINE ARTS
*Madonna and Child in the Clouds* (plate 57).

## FAENZA
### MUSEO CIVICO
*St Jerome* (plate 161b).

## FLORENCE
### BAPTISTERY
*Tomb of Pope John XXIII* (plates 52–53).
*Mary Magdalen* (plates 162–163).

### CASA MARTELLI
*The Martelli Family Shield* (plate 95).

### CHURCH OF ORSANMICHELE
*St Mark* (plates 6 and 8).
*St Peter* (plates 7 and 9).
*Tabernacle of St George* (plates 13 and 19–20).
*Tabernacle of the Parte Guelfa*, formerly part of *St Louis of Toulouse* (plates 30 and 36).

### CHURCH OF SAN LORENZO
Sculptural Decoration in the Old Sacristy:
*St Matthew* (plate 98a);
*St John* (plate 98b);
*St Luke* (plate 99a);
*St Mark* (plate 99b);
*St John on Patmos* (plate 100a);
*The Raising of Drusiana* (plate 100b);
*The Martyrdom of St John* (plate 101a);
*The Ascension of St John* (plate 101b);
*SS Cosmas and Damian* (plate 102a);
*SS Stephen and Lawrence* (plate 102b);
*Door of the Apostles* (plates 103a and 104–108);
*Door of the Martyrs* (plates 103b and 109–113);
*St Leonard* (plates 114–115);
*North Pulpit* (plates 178 and 180–191);
*South Pulpit* (plates 179 and 192–200).

### CHURCH OF SANTA CROCE
*Crucifix* (plate 39).
*Annunciation* (plates 88–94).

### DUOMO (SANTA MARIA DEL FIORE)
*First Prophet* (plate 1).
*Second Prophet* (plate 2).

*The Prophet Joshua* (plate 29).
*Bust of a Prophet* (plate 37a).
*Bust of a Sibyl* (plate 37b).

## MEDICI-RICCARDI PALACE
*Eight Tondi* (plates 214b and c and 215; attribution).

## MUSEO DELL'OPERA DEL DUOMO
*St John the Evangelist* (plates 10–12).
*Bearded Prophet* (plates 21–22).
*Prophet with a Scroll* (plates 23–24).
*Figure of a Prophet* (plate 25).
*Sacrifice of Isaac* (plates 26–27).
*The Prophet Jeremiah* (plates 50–51).
*The Prophet Habakkuk* (plates 72–73).
*Cantoria* (plates 74–82).

## MUSEO DELL'OPERA DI SANTA CROCE
*St Louis of Toulouse* (plates 30–35).

## MUSEO DI SANTO SPIRITO
*Two Doctors of the Church* (plate 150).

## MUSEO NAZIONALE (BARGELLO)
*Marble David* (plates 3–5).
*St George* (plates 13–18).
*The Marzocco* (plate 28).
*Bronze David* (plates 58–63).
*Two Bronze Heads* (plate 82).
*Atys-Amorino* (plates 96–97).
*Bust of a Youth* (plate 117).
*St John the Baptist* (plates 164–165).
*Head of a Man* (plate 177).
*St John the Baptist* (plate 204; attribution).
*Crucifixion* (plate 210; attribution).
*Madonna and Child* (plate 216a; attribution).
"*Niccolò da Uzzano*" (plate 218; attribution).
*Dancing Putto* (plate 220; attribution).

## PIAZZA DELLA SIGNORIA
*Judith and Holofernes* (plates 166–173 and color plate).

## UFFIZI GALLERY
*Bust of Homer* (plate 217b; attribution).

# LILLE
## LILLE MUSEUM, WICAR COLLECTION
*Dance of Salome* (plate 71).

# LONDON
## VICTORIA AND ALBERT MUSEUM
*The Ascension with Christ giving the Keys to St Peter* (plates 55–56).
*Bust of a Woman* (plate 202; attribution).
*Madonna and Child with Angels and Saints* (plate 203; attribution).
*Christ in the Sepulchre* (plate 205b; attribution).
*Madonna and Child* (plate 206a; attribution).
*Madonna* (plate 206b; attribution).
*Flagellation and Crucifixion* (plate 209; attribution).
*Lamentation* (plate 213; attribution).
*Nativity* (plate 214a; attribution).

# NAPLES
## CHURCH OF SANT'ANGELO A NILO
*Tomb of Cardinal Brancacci* (plate 54).

# PADUA
## BASILICA OF ST ANTHONY
*Crucifix* (plates 118–119).
Sculpture for the High Altar:
*Madonna and Child* (plates 102–123);
*St Francis* (plates 124a and 127–128);

*St Anthony* (plates 124b and 129);
*St Daniel* (plates 125a and 130);
*St Justina* (plates 125b and 131);
*St Louis* (plate 126a);
*St Prosdocimus* (plates 126b and 132–133);
*Miracle of the Mule* (plates 134 and 138);
*Miracle of the Speaking Babe* (plates 135 and 139);
*Miracle of the Penitent Son* (plates 136 and 140–141);
*Miracle of the Miser's Heart* (plates 137 and 142);
*Pietà* (plate 143);
*Symbols of the Evangelists* (plates 144–145);
*Singing and Musician Angels* (plates 146–148).
*The Deposition* (plate 149).

PIAZZA DEL SANTO

*Gattamelata Monument* (plates 151–159).

## PARIS

LOUVRE

*Crucifixion* (plate 208b; attribution).

MUSÉE JACQUEMART-ANDRÉ

*Figure of the Prophet* (plate 201; attribution).
*Martyrdom of St Sebastian* (plate 211; attribution).
*Portrait Bust of Marchese Ludovico III Gonzaga* (plate 217a; attribution).

## PISA

MUSEO NAZIONALE DI SAN MATTEO

*Bust of San Rossore* (plates 40–41).

## PRATO

DUOMO
*The Outside Pulpit* (plates 83–87).

## RALEIGH (NORTH CAROLINA)

NORTH CAROLINA MUSEUM OF ART

*Madonna and Child* (plate 216b; attribution).

## ROME

CHURCH OF SANTA MARIA IN ARACOELI

*Tomb of Archbishop Crivelli* (plate 70).

PRIVATE COLLECTION

*Madonna and Child* (plate 207a; attribution).

ST PETER'S BASILICA

*Tabernacle of the Sacrament* (plates 68–69).

## SIENA

BAPTISTERY

*Herod's Feast* (plates 42–45).
*Faith* (plate 46).
*Hope* (plate 47).
*Dancing Angel* (plate 48a).
*Angel with Trumpet* (plate 48b).

DUOMO

*Tomb of Bishop Pecci* (plate 49).
*St John the Baptist* (plates 174–176).

## TORRITA (SIENA)

MAESTRI HOSPITAL

*The Redeemer's Blood* (plate 212; attribution).

## VENICE

CHURCH OF SANTA MARIA DEI FRARI

*St John the Baptist* (plate 161a).

## WASHINGTON

NATIONAL GALLERY OF ART

*David* (plates 64–67).

# SELECTED CRITICISM

But when, after the long exile during which we, the Alberti, have become old, it was my good fortune to return to this beautiful native city of ours, I saw that you, Filippo, and our very good friend Donato the sculptor, and Nencio and Luca and Masaccio, had such talents for all praiseworthy things that not one of you could be considered inferior to any ancient and celebrated artist.

LEON BATTISTA ALBERTI,
*Della Pittura*, dedicated to Brunelleschi, 1436.

Donatello, also a Florentine, who excels for his talent and no less for his technique, is very well known for his bronze and marble figures, for he can make people's faces come to life, and in this he comes close to the glory of the ancient masters.

BARTOLOMEO FACIO,
*De viris illustribus*, 1456.

Donatello . . . for ever ready and lively in arranging his figures, which all seem to be moving, was a great imitator of the ancients and had an excellent understanding of perspective.

*Libro di Antonio Billi*, 1481–1530.

Donatello himself, said to have been a pupil of Cione, was highly praised for his bronze, wooden and marble sculptures. He alone has left us a larger number of works than all the other artists put together.

POMPONIO GAURICO,
*De Sculptura*, 1504.

In the days of our fathers there lived in Florence Donatello, a rare man who was simple in everything but his sculpture, in which many believe that no one has been greater than he. He executed many unusual objects and, talented though he was in his art, he was just as amenable and quick in expediting his many works, which can be admired to this day in several places.

PIETRO SUMMONTE,
*Letter to Marcantonio Michiel*, 1524.

It was very necessary to sculpture that Donatello should have worked so hard at all kinds of rounded figures, half-reliefs and *schiacciato* reliefs; for just as in the good days of the Ancient Greeks and Romans many artists made sculpture perfect, thus he alone, by the multiplicity of his works, made it perfect once more in our century. Artists should therefore acknowledge more greatness in this man than in any other born in our times.

GIORGIO VASARI,
*Le Vite*, 1550–68.

Apart from the fact that Donatello strictly observed all the rules of his art, he soared high because of his discreet and clear intelligence and his varied manner, which probably no one else had ever employed before. He gave us, in his *St George*, a work of such complete and rare beauty that it cannot fail to engender astonishment and wonder within our souls, for it hardly seems credible that it was modeled by a human hand.

FRANCESCO BOCCHI,
*Ragionamento sull'eccellenza della statua di San Giorgio di Donatello*, 1571–84.

Donatello was the first artist who not only departed from the traditional manner, for others had done this before him, but who, in so doing, created perfect works of exquisite value. He was an admirable emulator of the most ancient Greek sculptors and imparted to his figures a beautiful liveliness and authenticity.

FILIPPO BALDINUCCI,
*Notizie de' professori del disegno*, 1681.

Donatello appeared to seek every opportunity to let it be known that, being expert in the art of great compositions, no variety of subjects nor multiplicity of figures could frighten him. The small episodes which we admire in relief in the *Miracles of St Anthony*, whether on the main altar or on that of the Sacrament at Padua, prove how easily he could compose. The grandiose landscapes that he depicted in the backgrounds of his bas-reliefs, his knowledge of perspective, his intelligent way of stressing his foreground figures and his way of subtly indicating those in the background by sacrificing the less important details in favor of the essential ones, all these things he did magnificently. Furthermore, no one had ever taught him such refinements of art. He was indeed the first Italian genius to achieve such miracles of composition and distribution.

LEOPOLDO CICOGNARA,
*Storia della Scultura,* 1823.


All the praise bestowed upon Donatello by Vasari, Borghini and Baldinucci, who extol him as the first to restore sculpture to its rightful place among the arts, seems based upon the main fact that he was the first to impart to his figures that freedom of expression which later was to reach a climax with Buonarroti; and the Italians, because of the gloomy feeling that his figures inspired in them, called him *il terribile*. Ghiberti, who was his contemporary, and who had studied the most beautiful and varied spiritual attitudes, represented these attitudes in a moderate and well understood form of expression; Donatello, on the contrary, loved to portray an energetic and vital materiality, and in order to succeed in this direction, he expressed the less noble affections of the human spirit and soul.

KARL FRIEDRICH von RUMOHR,
*Italienische Forschungen,* 1827.


Donatello was a talented naturalist who knew no boundaries when it came to art. For him all that exists could be represented, plastically, and more than one subject was deemed by him to be worthy of representation merely because it existed and had a character of its own. For Donato the noblest task was to bring such a character to life in its crudest form and at times, when the subject warranted it, also in its full strength and grandiosity. He certainly did not lack a feeling for beauty, but beauty had to give way to character whenever character was called into question.

JACOB BURCKHARDT,
*Der Cicerone*, 1855.

Donatello is undoubtedly the greatest of Tuscan sculptors who preceded Michelangelo and, though far from achieving the latter's vigor and power of conception, he is certainly Buonarroti's superior when it comes to delicacy of touch, truth of detail, expression of character and skill of execution.

CHARLES C. PERKINS,
*Les Sculpteurs Italiens*, 1869.

Donatello's art as a portrait painter was the culminating moment of his realism. Both constitute one of the manifestations of the whole spirit of his time.

HANS SEMPER,
*Donatelli, seine Zeit und Schule*, 1875.

Finding himself torn between antiquity and reality, between the Pagan and the Christian, Donatello was more able than any of his contemporaries to reconcile principles and sentiments that appeared to be contradictory; he overcame those difficulties which his immediate successors, being perhaps more guided by science than enlightened with inspiration, entirely failed to conquer.

CAMILLO JACOPO CAVALLUCCI,
*Vita ed opere di Donatello*, 1886.

Donatello . . . faced the particular tasks of his epoch with a unique energy in which no one could rival him, and was never overwhelmed by the one-sidedness of unlimited realism. He portrayed men, and in so doing could pursue a characteristic form to the ultimate depth of ugliness, and then reflect once again, with assuredness and purity of vision, tranquil beauty, great beauty, enchanting beauty.

HEINRICH WÖLFFLIN,
*Classic Art*, 1898.

One may not like Donatello at all, but one must acknowledge him for what he has been. He should not be represented as a champion of the Renaissance, nor should one see in his works, which are so alive, a reflection of ancient statuary art. Whether he wanted it or not, Donatello's art represents the strongest protest ever made by an artist against the doctrines of antiquity.

MARCEL REYMOND,
*La sculpture Florentine*, 1898.

The first sculptor who could be described as a Renaissance artist in the fullest sense of the word is Donatello. Before Brunelleschi modeled the cupola of the Duomo, before Masaccio began his cycle of frescoes in the Carmine, Donatello had created, with his colossal statue of *St John* for the Duomo's façade and his *St George* in Orsanmichele, two plastic works of such importance that they became the guiding principles of sculpture for the greatest masters who were to follow him.

WILHELM von BODE,
*Denkmaeler der Renaissance-Skulptur Toscanas*, 1905.

If one compares it to that in Santa Croce, the *Crucifix* in the Church of the Santo illustrates how well the artist had studied Brunelleschi's lessons. The Man-God has offered himself to the holocaust; his mouth is grimacing with pain as he dies, his beautiful head is lowered, his last breath for the sake of humanity. The body is hanging lifeless from the cross. The energy displayed by the *Crucifix* in Santa Croce has gone, but the head, cloaked in the shadow of death, expresses his supreme anguish. The eyelids are closed upon the sunken eyes, the facial features have become sharpened, the mouth is half open, the hair seems to be dripping with blood, the ribs are visible beneath the skin.

ADOLFO VENTURI,
*Storia dell'arte. La scultura del Quattrocento*, 1908.

Like the marble *David*, *St George* is the image of youth defying its own destiny. . . . Donatello's *St George*, like (Verrocchio's) *Colleoni*, like Giorgione's *St Liberale*, expresses the Platonic idea of man at war. Like the *Doriphorus* of Polycleitus it carries within its marble the symbol of victorious strength.

ARDUINO COLASANTI,
*Donatello*, 1930.

Once he had mastered all the essentials, all the expressionistic potentialities of the Gothic language, and exhausted all the aspects and articulations of that language which had any significance for him, in a few works, intensely and briefly executed, Donatello changed his directions. With miraculous simplicity, tranquil assuredness and lucid fervor, he constructed upon those values . . . a marvellous new form, of unusual assertive power, impressive in its calm assuredness, elemental, essential, as felicitous and perfect as a force of nature: the *St George* at Orsanmichele.

CARLO LUDOVICO RAGGHIANTI,
*Donatello giovane*, 1933.

We must forget the Donatello of the minor works, of the busts, of the small bronzes, the Donatello of the *objets d'art*, just as we must forget Donatello, the primitive man and realistic artist, traditionally believed to have shouted: "Speak, speak, may your bowles drip blood!" In order to appreciate in full his historical greatness we must study the monumental sculptor, for that was what he really and exclusively was. We must go and examine his works *in situ*, as we do in the case of Ghiberti's masterpieces, and indeed, in his case it is even more important.

JENO LÁNYI,
*Problemi della critica Donatelliana*, 1939-40.

Donatello's sculpture is wholly unrelated to the classical ideal which discriminates between subjective and objective truth and, by guiding the former towards the latter, ensures a plastic *perfection* according to the empirical idea and resolves within a set of proportions the incidents of nature. The very value of the human figure is subordinated to the spatial feeling: it is revealed by the human episode. For this reason Donatello's drama is never an instrument for narration or composition, but is situated within the expression itself and explodes at the very moment in which it becomes fixed within a form.

GIULIO CARLO ARGAN,
*Il David di Donatello*, 1941.

A calculated indifference to execution, because of the distant effect in the light of free air is obvious, for instance, in the Olympia pediments. But in Donatello the very same effects are developed in terms of sculptural lights and chiaroscuri, and the result is fascinatingly complex and daring.

EMILIO CECCHI,
*Donatello*, 1943.

With the *Cantoria* Donatello created something new which had never been seen before his time. Confronted with this work we almost feel that it must have been executed by some other artist, who suddenly revealed himself and whose dominant quality was a form of decoration based entirely upon pictorial and chromatic elements. The problems with which Donatello struggled in his youth seem to have given way, here, to a different and extremely decorative style. The severity typifying his early statues, their *terribilità*, disappears before the vitality of this conception. The pictorial idea was an unknown joy to him as he modeled his previous works. Now it has taken full control.

LEO PLANISCIG,
*Donatello*, 1947.

It is seldom, I believe, that an artist feels as vigorously, desolately and dramatically about death as Donatello did. . . . This feeling was always present within him, and he expressed it in a variety of ways without necessarily selecting this or that particular subject in order to illustrate it more clearly: even in the lively and animated dances of *putti* in his pulpits at Florence and Prato, where everything should reflect the innocent joy of children at play, a simple gesture, a stress, a gleam of light or a darkening shadow can bring us suddenly back to the ever-present sense of drama which affected the artist's vision of the world and of human vicissitudes.

OTTAVIO MORISANI,
*Studi su Donatello*, 1952

Donatello's relationship with the classical world was not one of subjugation or of opposition; it derived, rather, from a free experience achieved by means other than those of humanistic sculpture. . . . In his *St John the Evangelist*, executed in 1415, a new and violent irruption of chiaroscuri breaks up the measured rhythm of the drapery, thereby creating an impetuous, irrepressible whirl of masses. Here, as in the *St Mark*, the tension of forms is justified by the new significance of Donatello's "naturalness": not energetic action, but the torment of an anxious effort towards self-knowledge. Confronted with this human drama, Donatello was to reform the whole of representational culture. The famous dispute about the *Crucifix* in Santa Croce, which probably took place in or about 1420, shows that Brunelleschi was alarmed and almost dismayed by the bold subversion that he was witnessing in the world of art and from which Donatello would emerge established as the perpetual critic, even of the new foundation, that is perspective, that he, Brunelleschi, had given to artistic expression.

An absolute, rational certainty; a mathematical abstraction; the number: all these factors were becoming the ideal principle of a new form, the model for which had been sought by the humanists within the realm of the classical era. Now, to Brunelleschi's technical studies—culminating in the schemes for geometrical representation of space which he had laid down in about 1425 in his two famous perspective tables, now lost—a new element was being added, that would justify and integrate for ever Filippo's principles. This new element was Donatello's immediate intuition.

L. BECHERUCCI,<br>
Enciclopedia Universale dell'Arte, 1958.

# BIBLIOGRAPHICAL NOTE

The bibliography concerning Donatello is vast. Up to 1913 we suggest M. Semrau, in *Kunstler-Lexicon*, by Thieme and Becker, Vol. IX (Leipzig, 1913) (under M. Semrau). An accurate index up to 1942 can be found at the end of R. Buscaroli's book: *L'arte di Donatello* (Florence, 1942). A further and very thorough bibliographical list may also be found in H. W. Janson's recent catalogue *The Sculpture of Donatello*, Vol. II, Princeton, 1957.

The following list, compiled in chronological order, includes all the essential texts and almost all the works which, in the present monograph, refer to the theories of the different authors. In our text, we have added to each name the date of the written work from which the theories have been quoted.

1472 (*c.*). A. MANETTI (?). *XIV uomini singhularj in Firenze dal 1400 innanzi*, Milanesi, Florence 1887.
1475 (*c.*). A. MANETTI. *Vita di Brunellesco*, E. Toesca, Florence 1927.
1495. LUCA LANDUCCI. *Diario fiorentino dal 1450 al 1516*, Jodoco del Badia, Florence 1883.
1510. F. ALBERTINI. *Memoriale di molte statue . . . di Florentia*, Florence (London 1909).
1530 (*c.*). A. BILLI. *Il libro di Antonio Billi*, Carl Frey, Berlin 1892.
1537–42. *Il codice magliabechiano*, Carl Frey, Berlin 1893.
1550 (*c.*). M. A. MICHIEL. *Notizia d'Opere di Disegno*, Frizzoni, Bologna 1884.
1550. *Le Vite*, first edition, published and edited by Corrado Ricci, Milan-Rome (no date).
1568. G. VASARI. *Le Vite de' più eccellenti pittori, scultori et architettori*, Milanesi, II, Florence 1906.
1584. F. BOCCHI. *Ragionamento sopra l'eccellenza della statue del San Giorgio di Donatello*, Florence 1584 (ed. P. Baroceni in *Trattati d'arte del Cinquecento*, III, 125–9, Bari 1962).
1584. F. BORGHINI. *Il Riposo*, Florence.
1591. F. BOCCHI. *Le bellezze della citta di Fiorenza*, Florence.
1677. F. BOCCHI. *Le bellezze di Firenze . . . ampliate da Giov. Cinelli*, Florence.
1881. F. BALDINUCCI. *Notizie de' Professori del Disegno*, V, Milan 1811.
1804–17. D. MORENI. *Memorie della Basilica di San Lorenzo*, Florence.
1823. L. CICOGNARA. *Storia della Scultura*, II, Prato.
1827. K. F. VON RUMOHR. *Italienische Forschunger*, II, Berlin (ed. J. von Schlosser, Frankfurt on the Main 1920).
1838–40. G. GAYE. *Carteggio inedito di artisti*, I, Florence.
1843. M. GUALANDI. *Memorie originali italiane risguardanti le belle arti*, Bologna.
1854. G. MILANESI. *Documenti per la storia dell'arte senese*, III, Siena.
1855. E. MÜNTZ. *Donatello*, Paris.
1866. L. PASSERINI. *Curiosità storico-artistiche fiorentine*, 1st series, Florence.
1869. C. G. PERKINS. *Les Sculpteurs Italiens*, I, Paris.

1875. H. SEMPER. *Donatello, seine Zeit und Schule,* Eitebberger, Vienna.
1877. C. TROMBETTA. *Donatello,* Rome.
1886. C. J. CAVALLUCCI. *Vita ed opere di Donatello,* Milan.
1866. A. SCHMARSOW. *Donatello,* Breslau.
1887. C. GUASTI. *Il Pergamo di Donatello pel Duomo di Prato,* Florence.
1887. G. MILANESI. *Catalogo delle opere di Donatello et bibliografia degli autori che ne hanno scritto,* Florence.
1887. H. SEMPER. *Donatellos Leben und Werke,* Innsbruck.
1887. H. VON TSCHUDI. "Donatello e la critica moderna," in *Rivista storica italiana.*
1888. D. GIVOLI. "Le opere di Donatello in Roma," in *Archivio Storico dell' Arte,* I, 24 ff.
1888. C. DE FABRICZY. "Les collections des Médicis au XVᵉ siècle," in *Archivio Storico dell'Arte,* I, 185 ff.
1888. E. MÜNTZ. *Les collections des Médicis au XVᵉ siècle,* Paris–London.
1891. M. SEMRAU. *Donatellos Kanzeln in S. Lorenzo,* Breslau.
1892–1905. W. BODE. *Denkmaeler der Renaissance-Skulptur Toscanas,* Munich.
1892. W. PASTOR. *Donatello,* Giessen.
1895. F. CORDENONS. *L'altare di Donatello,* Padua.
1895. A. GLORIA. *Donatello Fiorentino e le sue opere mirabili nel tempio di S. Antonio di Padova,* Padua.
1896. P. FRANCESCHINI. *L'Oratorio di San Michele in Orto,* Florence.
1896. G. B. GELLI. "Vite d'artisti," in *Archivio Storico Italiano,* XVI, 32 ff.
1897. C. BOITO. *L'Altare di Donatello e le altre opere nella Basilica Antoniana di Padova,* Milan.
1898. M. REYMOND. *La Sculpture Florentine,* I, Florence.
1899. C. DE MANDACH. *Saint Antoine de Padoue et l'art italien,* Paris.
1900. C. VON FABRICZY. "Donatellos Hl. Ludwig und sein Tabernakel an Orsanmichele," in *Jahrbuch der preussischen Kunstsammlungen,* XXI, 242 ff.
1903. LORD BALCARRES. *Donatello,* London.
1904. S. FECHHEIMER. *Donatello und die Reliefkunst,* Strasbourg.
1904. F. SCHOTTMÜLLER. *Donatello,* Munich.
1905. P. SCHUBRING. *Luca della Robbia,* Bielefeld–Leipzig.
1906. P. SCHUBRING. *Urbano da Cortona,* Cortona.
1907. P. SCHUBRING. *Donatello* (Klassiker der Kunst), Stuttgart–Leipzig.
1907. M. SEMRAU. "Donatello und die sogenannte Forzori Altar," in *Kunstwissenschaftliche Beitrage August Schmarsow gewidmet,* 95–102.
1908. A. G. MEYER. *Donatello,* Bielefeld–Leipzig.
1908. A. VENTURI. *Storia dell'Arte Italiana,* VI: *La scultura del quattrocento,* Milan.
1909. D. VON HADELN. "Ein Rekonstruktionversuch des Hochaltars Donatellos im Santo von Padua," in *Jahrbuch der preussischen Kunstsammlungen,* 35.
1909. G. POGGI. "Il Duomo di Firenze," in *Italienische Forschungen Kunsthistorisches Institut Florenz,* II, Berlin.
1910. E. BERTAUX. *Donatello,* Paris.
1910. W. BODE. *Florentiner Bildhauer der Renaissance,* Berlin.
1911. M. CRUTTWELL. *Donatello,* London.
1911. F. STUDNICZKA. *Das Bildnis Ciceros in der Renaissance,* Leipzig.

1924. G. DE FRANCOVICH. "Appunti su Donatello e Jacopo delle Quercia," in *Bollettino d' Arte*.
1924. F. STUDNICZKA. "Niccolò da Uzzano," in *Festschrift Wölfflin*, Munich.
1925. A. CHIAPPELLI. *Arte del Rinascimento*, Bologna.
[1927]. A. COLASANTI. *Donatello*, Rome. (No date.)
1927. G. FIOCCO. "I Lamberti a Venezia. II, Pietro di Niccolò Lamberti," in *Dedalo*, VIII, 362.
1927–29. M. DVORÀK. *Geschichte der Italienischen Kunst im Zeitalter der Renaissance*, Munich.
1929. P. BACCI. *Jacopo della Quercia*, Siena.
1929. E. KRIS. *Meister und Meisterwerke der Steinschneidekunst*, Vienna.
1930. G. FIOCCO. "Gli orecchioni dell'altare di Donatello al Santo," in *Il Santo*, 3 (1930), 21.
1930. L. PLANISCIG. *Piccoli bronzi italiani del Rinascimento*, Milan.
1932. G. FIOCCO. "Frammenti dell'altare di Donatello per il Santo di Padova," in *Padova*, VI, No. 1.
1932. L. GUIDALDI. *Il Santo*, IV, Padua, 241.
1932. E. MACLAGAN and M. H. LONGHURST. *Catalogue of Italian Sculpture in the Victoria and Albert Museum*, London.
1933. F. SCHOTTMÜLLER. *Die Bildwerke des Kaiser Friedrich Museum*, 2nd ed., Berlin–Leipzig.
1935. H. KAUFFMANN. *Donatello*, Berlin.
1935. J. LÁNYI. "Le statue quattrocentesche dei Profeti nel Campanile e nell'antica facciata di Santa Maria del Fiore," in *Rivista d' Arte*, XVII, 121 ff.
1935. J. LÁNYI. "Tre relievi inediti di Donatello," in *L' Arte*, XXXVIII, 284 ff.
1936. J. LÁNYI. "Zur Pragmatik der Florentiner Quattrocentoplastik (Donatello)," in *Kritische Berichte zur kunstgeschichtlichen Litteratur*, 1932–33, Leipzig.
1938. R. WITTKOWER. "A Symbol of Platonic Love . . . ," in *Journal of the Warburg Institute*, I, 260 ff.
1939. J. LÁNYI. "Problemi della critica Donatelliana," in *La Critica d' Arte*, XIX, Jan.–March, 9 ff.
1940. M. SALMI. *Donatello. Corso di Storia dell' Arte*, Part II, Florence.
1940–54. W. and E. PAATZ. *Die Kirchen von Florenz*, Frankfurt.
1941. G. C. ARGAN. "Il David di Donatello," in *Domus*, No. 2, 32.
1941. L. GOLDSCHEIDER. *Donatello*, London.
1942. R. BUSCAROLI. *L' Arte di Donatello*, Florence.
1942. E. CECCHI. *Donatello*, Rome.
1942. L. PLANISCIG. "I Profeti sulla porta della Mandorla del Duomo fiorentino," in *Rivista d' Arte*, XXIV, 125 ff.
1942. G. SWARZENSKI. In *Bulletin of the Museum of Fine Arts*, Boston, XL, 64 ff.
1947. L. PLANISCIG. *Donatello*, Florence.
1949. C. GALASSI. *La Scultura Fiorentina del Quattrocento*, Milan.
1949. J. POPE-HENNESSY. *Donatello's Relief of the Ascension* (Victoria and Albert Museum Monograph, No. 1), London.
1950. B. BEARZI. "Considerazioni di tecnica sul S. Ludovico e la Giuditta di Donatello," in *Bollettino d' Arte*, XXVI, 119 ff.
1950. A. CHASTEL. "Le jeune homme au camée platonicien del Bargello," in *Proporzioni*, III, 73 ff.

1950. P. SANPAOLESI. *La Sacrestia vecchia di San Lorenzo*, Pisa.

1950. P. VACCARINO. *Nanni di Banco*, Florence.

1950. W. R. VALENTINER. *Studies of Italian Renaissance Sculpture*, New York, 25 ff.

1951. O. MORISANI. *Michelozzo architetto*, Turin.

1951. P. TOESCA. *Il Trecento*, Turin.

1951. W. R. VALENTINER. "Notes on the early works of Donatello," in *The Art Quarterly*, 307 ff.

1951. W. VÖGE. "Donatello greift ein reimsiches Motif auf," in *Festschrift für Hans Jantzen*, 117 ff., Berlin.

1952 G. MARCHINI. "Di Maso di Bartolommeo e d'altri," in *Commentari*, III, 114 ff.

1952. O. MORISANI. *Studi su Donatello*, Venice.

1952. O. MORISANI. "Donatello, Agostino di Duccio ed altre sculture al Victoria and Albert," in *Bollettino di Storia dell'Arte, Magistero di Salerno*, II, 60.

1953. E. BERTI TOESCA. "Il cosiddetto Omero degli Uffizi," in *Bollettino d'Arte*, XXXVIII, Oct.–Dec., 307 ff.

1953. C. L. RAGGHIANTI. "Donatello giovane," 1933; re-published in *Sele-Arte, July-Aug.*

1954. G. WEISE. "Donatello und das Problem der Spätgotik," in *Zeitschrift für Kunstgeschichte*, XVII, 1954, 879–88.

1957. H. W. JANSON. *The Sculpture of Donatello*, Princeton, 2 vols.

1957 and 1958. V. MARTINELLI. "Donatello e Michelozzo a Roma," in *Commentari*, VIII, 167 ff.; IX, 3 ff.

1958. L. BECHERUCCI. "Donatello," in *Enciclopedia Universale dell'Arte*, IV, 404–18, Florence.

1959. M. GOSEBRUCH. "Florentinische Kapitelle von Brunelleschi bis zum Tempio Malatestiano und der Eigenstil der Frührenaissance," in *Römische Jahrbuch für Kunstgeschichte*, VIII, 63 ff.

1958. M. GOSEBRUCH. *Donatello. Das Reiterdenkmal des Gattamelata*, Stuttgart.

1958, M. LISNER. "Zur frühen Bildhauerarchitektur Donatellos," in *Münchner Jahrbuch der bildenden Kunst*, IX–X, 72 ff.

1959. G. KAUFFMANN. "Zu Donatellos Sängerkanzl," in *Mitteilungen des kunsthistorischen Institutes in Florenz*, I, 72 ff.

1959. I. LAVING. "The sources of Donatello's pulpits in San Lorenzo. Revival and freedom of choice in the early Renaissance," in *The Art Bulletin*, XLI, No. 1, 19 ff.

1959. A. PARRONCHI. "Le due tavole prospettiche del Brunelleschi," in *Paragone*, IX, No. 109, 3 ff.

1959. J. POPE-HENNESSY. "Some Donatello Problems," in *Studies in the History of Art. Dedicated to W. E. Suida*, 47 ff., London.

1959. J. POPE-HENNESSY. "The Martelli David," in *The Burlington Magazine*, CI, No. 673, 134 ff.

1959. W. R. VALENTINER. "Towards a chronology of Donatello's early works," in *Festschrift Friedrich Winkler*, 71 ff.

1959. M. WUNDRAM. "Donatello und Ciuffagni," in *Zeitschrift für Kunstgeschichte*, XXII, No. 2, 85 ff.

1961. C. DEL BRAVO. "Proposte e appunti per Nanni di Bartolo," in *Paragone*, XII, No. 137, 26 ff.

1961. G. FIOCCO. "L'Altare grande di Donatello al Santo," in *Il Santo*, 1, No. 1, 21 ff.

1961. G. PREVITALI. "Una data per il problema dei pulpiti di San Lorenzo," in *Paragone*, XII, No. 133, 48 ff.

1961. A. SARTORI. "Documenti riguardanti Donatello e il suo altare di Padova," in *Il Santo*, 1, No. 1, 37 ff.

1962. R. W. LIGHTBOWN. "Giovanni Chellini, Donatello and Antonio Rossellino," in *The Burlington Magazine*, XIV, No. 708, 102 ff.

1962. Catalogue of the Exhibition: *I bronzetti italiani del Rinascimento*, Florence.

1963. A. PARRONCHI. "Storia di una Gatta malata," in *Paragone*, 157, p. 60.

1963. G. CASTELFRANCO. *Donatello*, Milan.

# REPRODUCTIONS

## ACKNOWLEDGEMENT FOR
## PLATES

Most of the photographs in this book are extremely
recent: some, in fact, have never before been published. Most were provided by the Ditta Brogi di
Laurati of Florence. The remaining photographs are
from the following institutes and firms:

Gabinetto Fotografico della Sovraintendenza alle
Gallerie, Florence: 1, 2, 14, 15, 26b, 30–32, 37, 98–101,
103–113, 161b, 204, 215b; Alinari, Florence: 19b, 33,
54, 70, 75–81, 83, 95, 119, 212b–c, 213, 214; Staatliches Museen, Berlin: 38, 48c, 116, 160, 205a, 207b,
208a–c; Anderson, Rome: 49, 74, 118, 143–148, 151,
161a; Bulloz, Paris: 201, 208b, 210b, 215a; Victoria
and Albert Museum, London: 55, 56, 202, 203, 205b,
206, 209, 211, 212a; Museum of Fine Arts, Boston:
57; National Gallery of Art, Washington: 64–67;
Sansaini, Rome: 68–69; Giraudon, Paris: 71; North
Carolina Museum of Art, Raleigh, 214b; Private
Collections: 207a.
Material for all color plates was supplied by Scala,
Florence.

Plate 98. ST MATTHEW and ST JOHN, Florence, Old Sacristy of San Lorenzo

Plate 99. ST LUKE and ST MARK, Florence, Old Sacristy of San
Lorenzo

Plate 100. ST JOHN ON PATMOS and THE RAISING OF
DRUSIANA. Florence, Old Sacristy of San Lorenzo

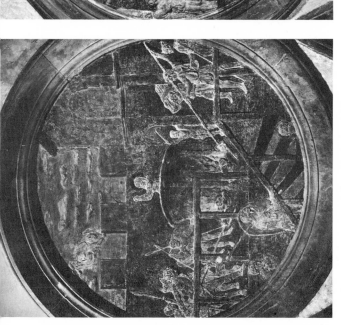

Plate 101. THE MARTYRDOM and THE ASCENSION OF ST JOHN,
Florence, Old Sacristy of San Lorenzo

Plate 102. SS COSMAS AND DAMIAN and SS STEPHEN AND
LAWRENCE. Florence, Old Sacristy of San Lorenzo

Plate 103. DOOR OF THE APOSTLES and DOOR OF THE MARTYRS, Florence, Old Sacristy of San Lorenzo

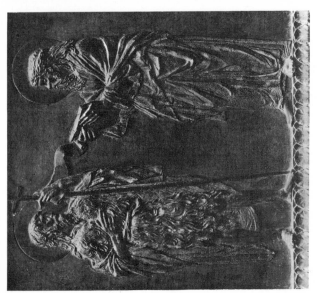

Plate 104. DOOR OF THE APOSTLES. *Detail*

Plate 105. DOOR OF THE APOSTLES. *Detail*

Plate 106. DOOR OF THE APOSTLES. *Detail*

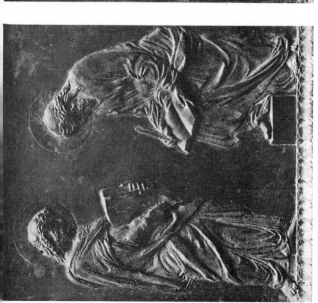

Plate 107. DOOR OF THE APOSTLES. *Detail*

Plate 108. DOOR OF THE APOSTLES. *Detail*

Plate 109. DOOR OF THE MARTYRS. *Detail*

Plate 110. DOOR OF THE MARTYRS. *Detail*

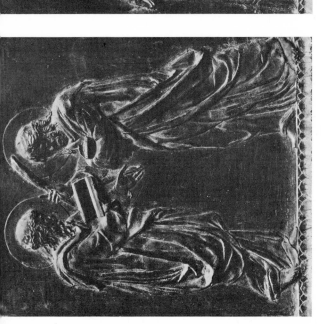

Plate III. DOOR OF THE MARTYRS. *Detail*

Plate 112. DOOR OF THE MARTYRS. *Detail*

Plate 113. DOOR OF THE MARTYRS. *Detail*

Plate 114. ST LEONARD, Florence, Old Sacristy of San Lorenzo

Plate 115. ST LEONARD, Florence, Old Sacristy of San Lorenzo

Plate 116. DAVID, Berlin, Staatliches Museen

Plate 117. BUST OF A YOUTH, Florence, Bargello

Plate 118. CRUCIFIX, Padua, Basilica of St Anthony

Plate 119. *Detail of plate 118*

Plate 120. MADONNA AND CHILD, Padua, Basilica of St Anthony

Plate 121. *Detail of plate 120*

Plate 122. *Detail of plate 120*

Plate 123. MADONNA AND CHILD. *Detail: rear of throne*

Plate 124. ST FRANCIS and ST ANTHONY, Padua, Basilica of St Anthony

Plate 125. ST DANIEL and ST JUSTINA, Padua, Basilica of St
Anthony

Plate 126. ST LOUIS and ST PROSDOCIMUS, Padua, Basilica of St Anthony

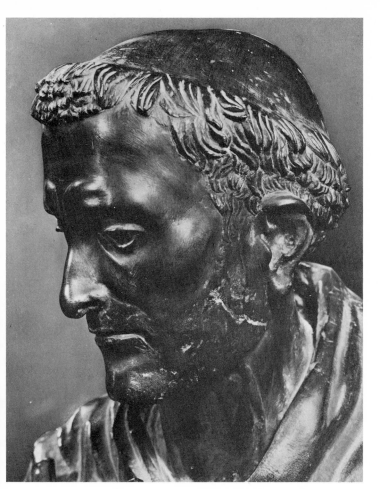

Plate 127. ST FRANCIS. *Detail*

Plate 128. ST FRANCIS. *Detail*

Plate 129. ST ANTHONY. *Detail*

Plate 130. ST DANIEL. *Detail*

Plate 131. ST JUSTINA. *Detail*

Plate 132. ST PROSDOCIMUS. *Detail*

Plate 133. ST PROSDOCIMUS. *Detail*

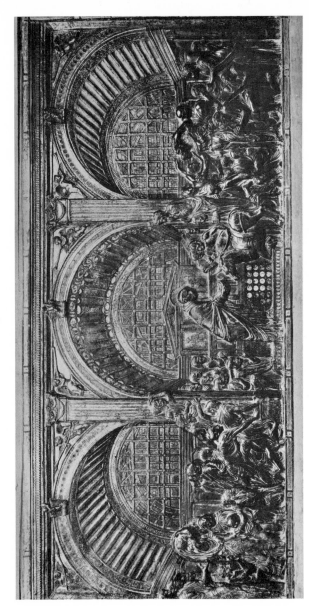

Plate 134. MIRACLE OF THE MULE, Padua, Basilica of St Anthony

Plate 135. MIRACLE OF THE SPEAKING BABE, Padua, Basilica of St Anthony

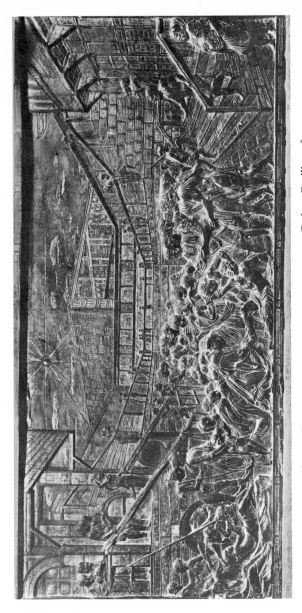

Plate 136. MIRACLE OF THE PENITENT SON, Padua, Basilica of
St Anthony

Plate 137. MIRACLE OF THE MISER'S HEART, Padua, Basilica of
St Anthony

Plate 138. *Detail of plate 134*

Plate 139. *Detail of plate 135*

Plate 140. *Detail of plate 136*

Plate 141. *Detail of plate 136*

Plate 142. *Detail of plate 137*

Plate 143. PIETÀ, Padua, Basilica of St Anthony

Plate 144. SYMBOLS OF THE EVANGELISTS: *St Matthew* and *St John*, Padua, Basilica of St Anthony

MARY MAGDALEN
(*detail of plate 162*)

Plate 145. SYMBOLS OF THE EVANGELISTS: *St Mark* and *St Luke*,
Padua, Basilica of St Anthony

Plate 146. SINGING AND MUSICIAN ANGELS, Padua, Basilica of
St Anthony

Plate 147. SINGING AND MUSICIAN ANGELS, Padua, Basilica of
St Anthony

Plate 148. SINGING AND MUSICIAN ANGELS, Padua, Basilica of St Anthony

Plate 149. THE DEPOSITION, Padua, Basilica of St Anthony

Plate 150. TWO DOCTORS OF THE CHURCH, Florence, Museo
di Santo Spirito

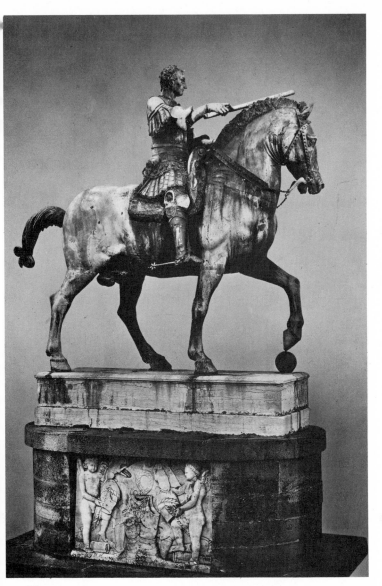

Plate 151. GATTAMELATA MONUMENT, Padua, Piazza del Santo

Plate 152. GATTAMELATA MONUMENT. Padua, Piazza del Santo

Plate 153. GATTAMELATA MONUMENT. Padua, Piazza del Santo

Plate 154. GATTAMELATA MONUMENT. Padua, Piazza del Santo

Plate 155. *Detail of plate 154*

Plate 156. *Detail of plate 154*

Plate 157. *Detail of plate 154*

Plate 158. *Detail of plate 154*

Plate 159. *Detail of plate 154*

Plate 160. ST JOHN THE BAPTIST, formerly in Berlin, Staatliches
Museen

JUDITH AND HOLOFERNES
*(detail of plate 166)*

Plate 161. ST JOHN THE BAPTIST, Venice, Church of Santa
Maria dei Frari, *and* ST JEROME, Faenza, Museo Civico

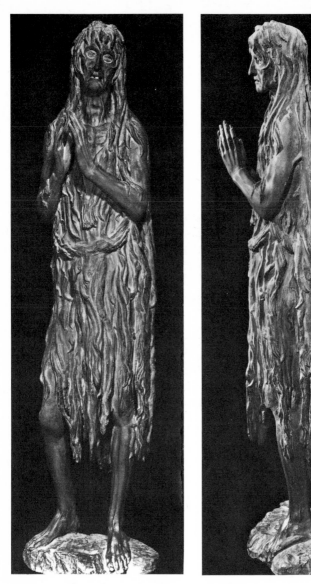

Plate 162. MARY MAGDALEN, Florence, Baptistery

Plate 163. *Detail of plate 162*

Plate 164. ST JOHN THE BAPTIST, Florence, Bargello

Plate 165. *Detail of plate 164*

Plate 166. JUDITH AND HOLOFERNES, Florence, Piazza della
Signoria

Plate 167. JUÐITH AND HOLOFERNES

Plate 168. *Detail of plates 166–167*

Plate 169. *Detail of plates 166–167*

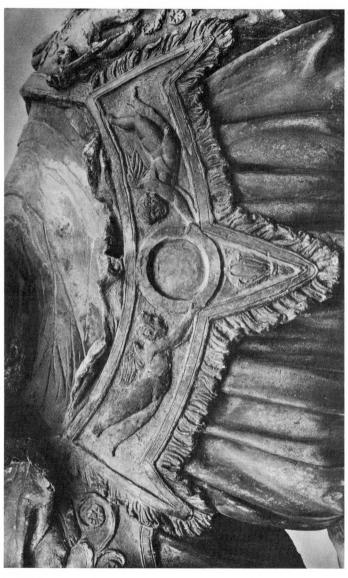

Plate 170  Detail of plates 166–167

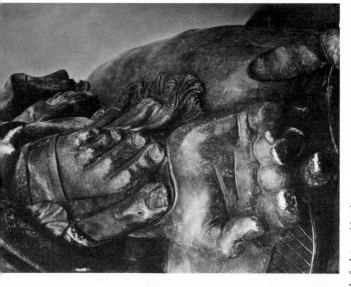

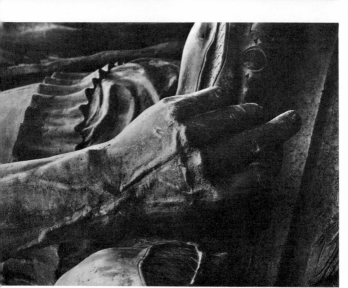

Plate 171. *Detail of plates 166–167*

Plate 172. *Detail of plates 166–167*

Plate 173. *Detail of plates 166–167*

Plate 174. ST JOHN THE BAPTIST, Siena, Duomo

Plate 175. *Detail of plate 174*

Plate 176. *Detail of plate 174*

Plate 177. HEAD OF A MAN, Florence, Bargello

Plate 178. NORTH PULPIT, Florence, Church of San Lorenzo

Plate 179. SOUTH PULPIT, Florence, Church of San Lorenzo

Plate 180. *Detail of plate 178*

Plate 181. *Detail of plate 178.* The Agony in the Garden

Plate 182. *Detail of plate 178.* Christ before Caiaphas

Plate 183. *Detail of plate 178*. Christ before Pilate

Plate 184. *Detail of plate 178.* Crucifixion

Plate 185. *Detail of plate 178*. The Descent from the Cross

Plate 186. *Detail of plate 185*

Plate 187. *Detail of plate 185*

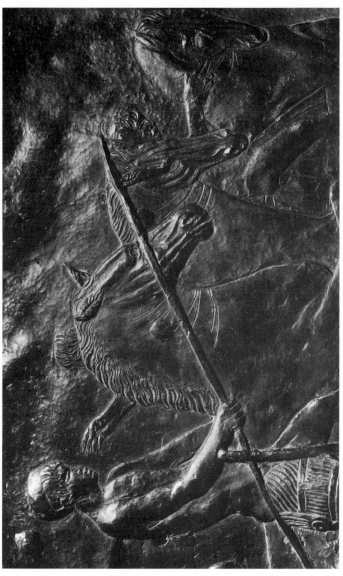

Plate 188. *Detail of plate 185*

Plate 189. *Detail of plate 185*

Plate 199. *Detail of plate 178. Deposition*

Plate 191. *Detail of plate 190*

Plate 192. *Detail of plate 179*. Three Women at the Tomb

Plate 193. *Detail of plate 179*. The Descent into Limbo

Plate 195. *Detail of plate 179. The Ascension*

Plate 196. *Detail of plate 179.* Pentecost

Plate 197. *Detail of plate 179.* The Martyrdom of St Lawrence

Plate 198. *Detail of plate 194*

Plate 199. *Detail of plate 197*

OPVS
DONATELL
FLO

Plate 200. *Detail of plate 179*: the frieze

Plate 201. FIGURE OF A PROPHET, Paris, Musée Jacquemart-André (attribution)

Plate 202. BUST OF A WOMAN, London, Victoria and Albert
Museum (attribution)

Plate 203. MADONNA AND CHILD WITH ANGELS AND SAINTS,
London, Victoria and Albert Museum (attribution)

Plate 204. ST JOHN THE BAPTIST, Florence, Museo Nazionale
del Bargello (attribution)

Plate 205. FLAGELLATION, formerly Berlin, Staatliches Museen, *and* CHRIST IN THE SEPULCHRE, London, Victoria and Albert Museum (attributions)

Plate 206. MADONNA AND CHILD *and* MADONNA, London, Victoria and Albert Museum (attributions)

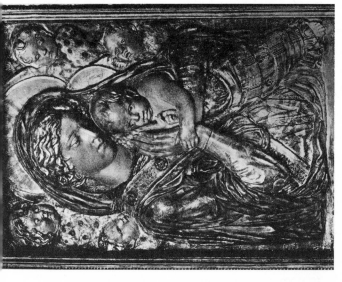

Plate 207. MADONNA AND CHILD, Rome, Private Collection, *and* MADONNA AND CHILD WITH FOUR CHERUBS, formerly Berlin, Staatliches Museen (attributions)

Plate 208. CRUCIFIXION, Berlin, Staatliches Museen, CRUCI-
FIXION, Paris, Louvre, *and* FLAGELLATION, formerly Berlin,
Staatliches Museen (attributions)

Plate 209. FLAGELLATION AND CRUCIFIXION, London,
Victoria and Albert Museum (attribution)

Plate 210. CRUCIFIXION, Florence, Bargello (attribution)

Plate 211. MARTYRDOM OF ST SEBASTIAN, Paris, Musée Jacquemart-André (attribution)

Plate 212. THE REDEEMER'S BLOOD, Torrita, Maestri Hospital
(attribution)

Plate 213. LAMENTATION, London, Victoria and Albert Museum
(attribution)

Plate 214. NATIVITY, London, Victoria and Albert Museum, *and* TONDI, Florence, Medici-Riccardi Palace (attributions)

Plate 215. TONDI, Florence, Medici-Riccardi Palace (attributions)

Plate 216. MADONNA AND CHILD, Florence, Bargello *and* MADONNA AND CHILD, Raleigh, North Carolina Museum of Art (attributions)

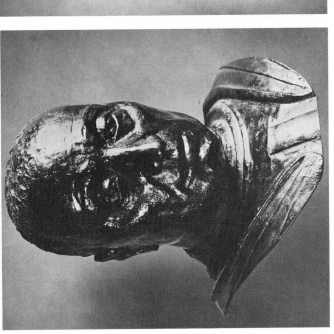

Plate 217. PORTRAIT BUST OF MARCHESE LUDOVICO III
GONZAGA, Paris, Musée Jacquemart-André, *and* BUST OF HOMER,
Florence, Uffizi (attributions)

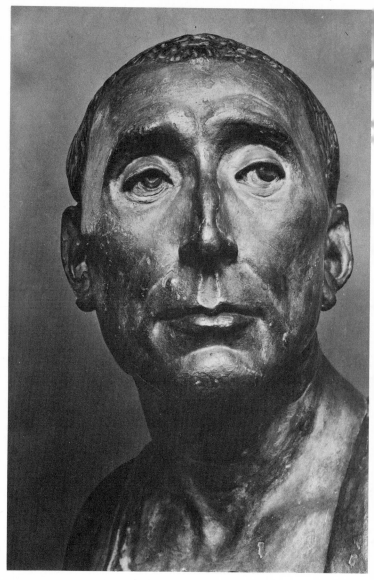

Plate 218. "NICCOLÒ DA UZZANO," Florence, del Bargello
(attribution)

Plate 219. BAPTISM OF CHRIST, Arezzo Cathedral (attribution)

Plate 220. DANCING PUTTO, Florence, Bargello (attribution)